A Pleasury of
Witticisms and
Word Play

A Pleasury of Witticisms and Word Play

ANTONY B. LAKE

Cartoon illustrations by Harold Montiel

HART PUBLISHING COMPANY, INC.
NEW YORK CITY

Contents

A Pleasury of Witticisms and Word Play

Alliterative Rhymes

Here is a selection of *tours de force* concocted by some of our wilier versifiers.

Cardinal Wolsey was the son of a butcher. With his rapid rise to political eminence, he managed to draw an unhealthy quota of jealous antagonists. William Pitt made capital of Wolsey's humble origin by lampooning him in these lines:

Begot by butchers, but by butchers bred,
How high His Highness holds his haughty head.

A couple of centuries ago, the medical profession was not held in high repute—perhaps with good cause. Here are some anonymous lines that reflect the temper of the day:

Medical men my mood mistaking,
Most mawkish, monstrous messes making,
Molest me much.
More manfully my mind might meet my malady.
Medicine's mere mockery murders me.

Addressed to the same group, here are some playful lines:

I need not your needles,
  They're needless to me;
For kneading of needles
  Were needless you see.

9

> *But did my neat trousers*
> *But need to be kneed—*
> *I then should have need*
> *Of your needles, indeed!*

David Garrick, likely the most famous English actor of the 18th century, patronized an apothecary and physician by the name of Dr. John Hill. When Hill died, Garrick penned his obituary in the following lines:

> *For physic and farces*
> *His equal there scarce is;*
> *His farces are physic,*
> *His physic a farce is!*

But it took one Mr. Poulter, a resident of Winchester, England, to top all previous efforts. He composed what is probably the longest alliterative poem on record. Poulter ran the full gamut from A to Z, as witness the following:

> *An Austrian army, awfully arrayed,*
> *Boldly by battery, besieged Belgrade.*
> *Cossack commanders cannonading come*
> *Dealing destruction's devastating doom.*
> *Every endeavor engineers essay*
> *For fame, for fortune, forming furious fray.*
> *Gaunt gunners grapple, giving gashes good,*
> *Heaves high his head, heroic hardihood.*
> *Ibraham, Islam, imps in ill,*

10

Alliterative Rhymes

Jostle John Jarovlitz, Jem, Joe, Jack, Jill;
Kick kindling Kutosoff, king's kinsmen kill.
Labor low levels loftiest, longest lines.

Men march mid moles, mid mounds, mid murd'rous
  mines,
Now nightfall's near; now needful nature nods,
Opposed, opposing, overcoming odds,
Poor peasants, partly purchased, partly pressed,
Quite quaking, quarter, quarter quickly quest.
Reason returns, recalls redundant rage,
Saves sinking soldiers, softens Signiors sage.
Truce, Turkey, truce, treacherous Tartar train,
Unwise, unjust unmerciful Ukraine,
Vanish vile vengeance, vanish victory vain.
Wisdom wails war, wails warring words.
Xerxes, Xanthippus, Ximines, Xavier,
Yet Yassey's youth ye yield your youthful yest,
Zealously, zanes, zealously, zeals zest.

Anagrams & Palindromes

An anagram is, plain and simple, a rearrangement of the letters of a word or words to make another word or words. The word SMILE, for example, yields the anagram *slime,* as well as *miles* and *limes.*

One of the earliest and best-known anagrams was created from the question that Pilate asked Jesus:

Quid est veritas? [What is truth?]

THE ANSWER:
Est vir qui adest. [It is the man who is here.]

Here are some other unusually apt anagrams:

THE EYES	*They see.*
A SHOPLIFTER	*Has to pilfer.*
THE COUNTRYSIDE	*No city dust here!*
THE MONA LISA	*No hat, a smile.*
THE NUDIST COLONY	*No untidy clothes!*
THE UNITED STATES OF AMERICA	*Attaineth its cause: freedom!*

Many have been frustrated by the tricky task of making one word out of *new door.* If the solution eludes you, see the bottom of page 14.

Anagrams have inspired linguistic jugglers to various creative efforts, for better or verse. To wit:

A VILE *young lady* on EVIL *bent,*
Lowered her VEIL *with sly intent.*
"LEVI," *she said,* "*It's time to play.*
What shall we do to LIVE *today?*"
"*My dear,*" *said he,* "*do as you please.*
"*I'm going to eat some* IVEL *cheese!*"

(Ivel cheese is a fictitious *fromage* made in the valley
of the non-existent Ivel river.)

Consider the following quatrain in which the letters P T S and O have been used to form five different
words:

Oh, landlord, fill our thirsting POTS,
Until the TOPS *flow over;*
Tonight, we STOP *upon this* SPOT,
Tomorrow, POST *for Dover.*

An anagram that reads the same backwards and

forwards—the word *toot*, for instance—is called a palindrome.

The story goes that the first palindrome ever fashioned was uttered by the first man. Adam allegedly introduced himself to Eve thus:

"MADAM, I'M ADAM."

Here are a few small ones:

STEP ON NO PETS.

LIVE NOT ON EVIL.

DRAW, O COWARD!

'TIS IVAN ON A VISIT.

WAS IT A RAT I SAW?

One word.

14

YREKA BAKERY

*(an actual bakery at
322 W. Miner St., Yreka, California)*

A palindrome of great historical interest is the classic supposedly uttered by Napoleon:

"ABLE WAS I ERE I SÁW ELBA."

A palindrome that might be instrumental in celebrating a Black Mass is this exhortation to Satan:

LIVE, O DEVIL! REVEL EVER! LIVE! DO EVIL!

And here's one that offers a revolutionary method for keeping trim:

DOC, NOTE I DISSENT: A FAST NEVER PREVENTS
A FATNESS. I DIET ON COD.

But undoubtedly the cleverest palindrome ever penned in English was the work of some anonymous genius who apotheosized the Panama Canal in seven words which, however you look at them, yield the same pithy statement:

A MAN, A PLAN, A CANAL—PANAMA!

Appropriate Adverbs

"I wish I'd made that bet," said the bookmaker, hoarsely.

⁂

"Do you think you understand my painting?" asked Picasso, artfully.

⁂

"Bing Crosby might get a sore throat," said Bob, hopefully.

"What an ample bosom!" he remarked, robustly.

⁂

"But I don't want a spaniel, I want a corgi," said the pet-fancier, doggedly.

"Your drip-dries are crumpled," said the laundress, ironically.

※

"I only want 20,000 machine guns," said the dictator, disarmingly.

※

"This is an imitation diamond," said the dealer, stonily.

※

"I practiced three hours on my guitar," said the folk singer, pluckily.

※

"Dear Sirs, please send me your catalogue," he wrote, listlessly.

※

"These pants are not short enough," said the young girl, hotly.

※

"I wasn't there," she remarked, absently.

※

"I must attend to my flock," said the vicar, sheepishly.

"My Chinese necklace has been stolen," she said, jadedly.

※

"How do you like my petticoat?" she asked, shiftlessly.

※

"I am on the wrong street," said the Frenchman, ruefully.

※

"I have flunked this lousy exam," said the student, testily.

※

"My aim is true," said the swordsman, pointedly, as he lunged toward his opponent.

※

"Have you anything by Hugo?" asked Les, miserably.

※

"I've $400.00, any more?" asked the auctioneer, morbidly.

※

"I don't *have* to do this for a living," she said, tartly.

※

"May I leave the room?" asked the schoolboy, highhandedly.

"This ain't real turtle soup!" the woman said, mockingly.

※

"He resembles a goat!" he chortled, satirically.

※

"My pencil is dull," he remarked, pointlessly.

"I tore his valentine in two," she said, halfheartedly.

※

"Press your own shirt!" she declared, flatly.

※

"I'll drive the truck," he whispered, shiftily.

※

"Yes, I've read *Gulliver's Travels*," he replied, swiftly.

"I work as a ditch-digger," he announced, trenchantly.

※

"We're out of pumpernickel," the baker said, wryly.

※

"Have you ever read Voltaire?" the teacher asked, candidly.

※

"My dime rolled into the sewer," the boy cried, gratefully.

※

"A mule is half donkey and half horse," he explained, crossly.

※

"You still haven't learned how to bake," her husband sneered, crustily.

※

"I hate shellfish!" she snapped, crabbedly.

※

"My glands are swollen," she said, mumpishly.

※

"My dog is terribly ill," the boy shouted, rabidly.

"I've got all the work I can handle," the doctor said, patiently.

※

"I'll cut him to ribbons!" she scowled, mincingly.

※

"I wish I could remember the name of that card game," she said, wistfully.

"I slept in a draft last night," he remarked, stiffly.

※

"I can't stand strawberries," she said, rashly.

※

"May he rest in peace," the minister intoned, gravely.

Classic Dedications

Vice President Tom Marshall dedicated his memoirs:
To President Woodrow Wilson, from his only Vice.

Franklin P. Adams inscribed one volume of verse:
To my loving wife, but for whose constant inter-
ruptions, this book would have been finished six
months earlier.

☀

Carl Winston dedicated How to Turn a Million into a
Shoestring *thus:*
I should be remiss, indeed, if I failed to acknowl-
edge my indebtedness to the People's Bank of
Bridgeport, the Connecticut Light and Power Co.,

the New England Telephone Co., Sears Roebuck, Casey Fuel, the West Redding Market, the Internal Revenue Department, and another creditor whose name is Morris H. Legion. The total is $17,886.05. Hi, Fellows!

※

Inscription on a cigarette lighter:
To My Matchless Wife.

※

Al Jaffee of Mad *Magazine dedicated one of his books:*
To myself, without whose inspired and tireless efforts this book would not have been possible.

※

An RKO director dedicated his first book:
To my wife, without whose absence this could not have been written.

※

Inez McEwen dedicated her book So This Is Ranching:
To my infant grandson, the only gent on whom I've been able to pin anything.

Classic Stanzas

These verses are all well known, either for their brevity or their wit, which in some cases amount to the same thing.

ODE ON THE ANTIQUITY OF FLEAS

Adam
Had 'em!

※

ONTOLOGICAL REFLECTION ON THE MEANING
OF EXISTENCE

I—
Why?

※

ODE ON THE CONDITION OF THE UNITED STATES
AFTER SEVERAL YEARS OF PROHIBITION

Wet
Yet.

※

Sir, I admit your general rule,
That every poet is a fool:
But you yourself may serve to show it,
That every fool is not a poet.

Alexander Pope

24

Classic Stanzas

ODE TO THE BRAHMINS OF BOSTON

Here's to dear old Boston,
    The home of the bean and the cod;
Where the Lowells speak only to Cabots,
    And the Cabots speak only to God.

᠅

ODE TO THE CITY OF COLOGNE

In Köln, a town of monks and bones,
And pavements fanged with murderous stones,
And rags, and hags, and hideous wenches,
I counted two-and-seventy stenches,
All well defined, and separate stinks!
Ye nymphs that reign o'er sewers and sinks,
The river Rhine, it is well known,
Doth wash your city of Cologne;
But tell me, nymphs, what power divine
Shall henceforth wash the river Rhine?

        Samuel Taylor Coleridge

᠅

Lives of great men oft remind us
    As we o'er their pages turn
That we, too, may leave behind us
    Letters that we ought to burn.

        Thomas Hood

25

I do not love thee, Doctor Fell,
The reason why I cannot tell,
But this one thing I know full well:
I do not love thee, Doctor Fell.

Thomas Brown

A Christian is a man who feels
   Repentance on a Sunday
For what he did on Saturday
   And is going to do on Monday.

Thomas Russell Ybarra

OH, TO BE IN ENGLAND NOW THE WEATHER'S THERE!

Ah, lovely Devon . . .
Where it rains eight days out of seven!

Sir Christopher Wren
Said, "I am going to dine with some men.
If anybody calls
Say I am designing St. Paul's."

※

O what a tangled web we weave
When first we practice to deceive!
But when we've practiced quite a while
How vastly we improve our style!

J. R. Pope

※

Great fleas have little fleas upon their back to bite 'em;
And little fleas have lesser fleas, and so *ad infinitum*.

※

Seven wealthy towns contend for Homer dead;
Through which the living Homer had to beg his bread.

※

ODE TO MARRIAGE

'Tis better to have loved and lost,
Than wed and be forever bossed.

※

WORLD WAR I

The general got the croix-de-guerre—
And the son of a bitch was never there.

REFLECTIONS OF A JADED LOVER

When you're away, I'm restless, lonely,
Wretched, bored, dejected; only
Here's the rub, my darling dear,
I feel the same when you are near.

Sam Hoffenstein

ODE TO A PREACHER

I never see my rector's eyes,
He hides their light divine;
For when he prays, he shuts his own,
And when he preaches, mine.

❋

"Come, come," said Tom's father, "at your time of life,
There's no longer excuse for thus playing the rake—
It is time you should think, boy, of taking a wife."
"Why so it is, father—whose wife shall I take?"

Thomas Moore

REFLECTIONS ON A PICNIC

Upon this theme I'll briefly touch:
Too far to go to eat too much.

※

SWAN SONG

Swans sing before they die—
'Twere no bad thing
Should certain persons die
Before they sing.

※

ODE TO YESTERYEAR

The good old days, the good old days,
We all so fondly speak of;
Which, if they ever should come back,
No one could stand a week of.

※

REFLECTIONS ON THE GRAPE

If all be true that I do think,
There are five reasons we should drink;
Good wine—a friend—or being dry—
Or lest we should be by and by—
Or any other reason why.

Henry Aldrich

WORLD WAR III

I won't print and you won't see
The verses written on World War III.

❄

REFLECTIONS ON HIGHWAY TRAVEL

Wherever the place,
Whatever the time;
Every lane moves
But the one where I'm.

Ethel B. DeVito

REFLECTIONS ON BACHELORHOOD

A bachelor is a cagey guy
And has a load of fun:
He sizes all the cuties up
And never Mrs. one.

John Wycherly

ODE ON GARRULITY

Whene'er a hen lays eggs, with each
She is impelled to make a speech.
The selfsame urge stirs human bones
Whenever men lay cornerstones.

❊

REFLECTIONS ON A DOUGHNUT

'Twixt the optimist and the pessimist
The difference is droll:
The optimist sees the doughnut
While the pessimist sees the hole.

❊

ON LOVE

Love is like an onion
You taste it with delight,
And when it's gone you wonder
What ever made you bite.

❊

PHILOSOPHICAL REFLECTION ON AGING

King David and King Solomon
Lived merry, merry lives,
With many, many lady friends
And many, many wives;
But when old age crept onward,
With all its many qualms,
King Solomon wrote the Proverbs
And King David wrote the Psalms.

LIFE'S SHORTEST STORY

The saddest words of tongue or pen
Perhaps may be "It might have been."
The sweetest words we know, by heck,
Are simply these: "Enclosed find check."

※

When two egotists meet
It results in a tie:
A vocal dead heat,
With an I for an I.

※

For a time newspapers across the country partici-
pated in an informal contest to see who could devise
the cleverest verse offering advice to motorists. The following ditties were gleaned from among the best.

Oh shed a tear
For Luther Stover;
He tried to toot
Two State cops over.

He who stops to look each way
Will drive his car another day.
But he who speeds across the "stop"
Will land in some mortician's shop.

And he who starts his car in gear
May end his ride upon a bier.
And he who crashes through the red
May wake up once and find he's dead.

Bill Muffet said
 His car couldn't skid;
This monument shows
 It could and did.

Please wail one wail
 For Adolph Barr;
He just would drive
 A one-eyed car.

33

Classroom Boners

The original "Classroom Boner" (or as the British say, "Schoolboy Howler") probably dates back to the day that some dumb pupil first touched quill to parchment. Today, these blunders continue to pour forth in great numbers; there seems to be no end to the droll twists students can unintentionally give to the simplest facts.

There is scarcely a teacher in the land who has failed to collect choice specimens of this artless art. What follows is a collection of some of the most priceless student errors ever penned. Each one is an authentic blunder, not a made-up wisecrack—as the utter absurdity of these gems will readily demonstrate.

To collect fumes of sulphur, hold a deacon over a flame in a test tube.

Although the patient had never been fatally ill before, he woke up dead.

The invention of the steamboat caused a network of rivers to spring up.

Geometry teaches us to bisex angels.

If one angle of a triangle is more than 90 degrees the triangle is obscene.

Germany is an industrial country because the poor have nothing to do so they make lots and lots of factories.

A polygon with seven sides is called a hooligan.

The best way to eat cream cheese and lox is with a beagle.

※

A triangle inside a circle is called a circumcised triangle.

※

Zanzibar is noted for its monkeys. The British Governor lives there.

※

What's a myth?
A myth's a female moth.

※

Shakespeare wrote tragedies, comedies and errors.

Rural life is found mostly in the country.

※

A cascade is a drink like lemonade that is made in a cask.

※

Chaucer was a great English poet who wrote many poems and verses and sometimes wrote literature.

The general direction of the Alps is up.

※

A octopus is a person who hopes for the best.

※

Algebraical symbols are used when you do not know what you are talking about.

When you breathe you inspire. When you do not breathe you expire.

The people of Uganda don't wear much clothing; they dress like statues.

Horace Greeley was the worst defeated candidate ever elected.

To pick up courage, he whistled in the dark. After he thus buoyed himself up, he felt like a boy—no longer a child.

A glacier is a man who goes along the street with glass in his hand and puts it in windows.

Napoleon had three children, not one of whom lived to maternity.

❊

A martyr is a pile of wood set on fire with a man on top.

❊

Unleavened bread is bread made without any ingredients.

❊

There were no wars in Greece, as the mountains were so high they couldn't climb over to see what their neighbors were doing.

The Pawnees were a tribe that ran hockshops for Indians.

In many states, murderers are put to death by electrolysis.

※

A sincere friend is one who says nasty·things to your face, instead of saying them behind your back.

Columbus was a great navigator who cursed about the Atlantic.

※

When there are no fresh vegetables you can always get canned.

※

The difference between a king and a president is that a king is the son of his father, but a president isn't.

※

Owing to slackness of demand there was a great slut on the market.

A virgin forest is a forest in which the hand of man has never set foot.

※

A bibliomaniac is a person who reads the Bible incessantly from cover to cover.

※

Burlesque is a kind of take-off.

※

The two genders are masculine and feminine. The masculines are divided into temperate and intemperate, and feminines into frigid and torrid.

※

Letters in sloping type are in hysterics.

Floods from the Mississippi may be prevented by putting big dames in the river.

Please rush my allowance. I have fallen into errors with my landlady.

At three years of age my father was killed in the war.

Dated coffee is coffee brewed from dates.

The family group consisted of three adults and six adultresses.

Harold mustarded his men before the Battle of Hastings.

Imports are ports very far inland.

A census taker is a man who goes from house to house increasing the population.

Bismarck, the father of the Kaiser, was very fond of herring.

❋

Write what you know of the Last Supper.
I was away for that. I had the measles.

❋

When a man has more than one wife he is a pigamist.

❋

The process of turning steam into water again is called conversation.

Trigonometry is when a lady marries three men at the same time.

※

Acrimony is what a man gives his divorced wife.

※

Chivalry is the attitude of a man toward a strange woman.

※

In Christianity a man can only have one wife. This is called monotony.

※

To be a good nurse you must be absolutely sterile.

A Shintoist is an original dancer who shakes his shins and his toes.

The Indian squabs carry porpoises on their backs.

Magna Carta provided that no free man should be hanged twice for the same offense.

What would you do in the case of a man bleeding from a wound in the head?

I would put a tourniquet around his neck.

What is the chief cause of divorce?
  Marriage.

Ceylon is jointed to India by a chain of coral wreathes.

S.O.S. is a musical term meaning same only softer.

Herrings go about the sea in shawls.

Emphasis in reading is putting more distress in one place than another.

Illegal parking is staying longer than you should in a place where you are not allowed to stay at all.

The benefit of longitude and latitude is that when a man is drowning he can call out what latitude and longitude he is in and we can find him.

※

Homer was not written by Homer but by another man of that name.

※

A morality play is a play in which the characters are goblins, ghosts, virgins, and other supernatural creatures.

※

Carton was doing something he had never done before —dying for someone else.

The Pilgrim Fathers were Adam and Eve.

The Trojans rode a wooden horse that said, "Beware the Greeks, asking for lifts."

※

A psalmist is one who tells fortune by reading hands.

※

Armadillo is the Spanish navy which defeated the Duke of Wellington.

※

Two popular ancient sports were Antony and Cleopatra.

※

Robert Louis Stevenson got married and went on his honeymoon. It was then he wrote *Travels with a Donkey*.

Joseph Haydn had a lot of will power; he died in 1809 and is still dead.

※

An executive is the man who puts murderers to death.

※

One of the most popular fugues was the one between the Hatfields and the McCoys.

※

Mata Hari means suicide in Japanese.

※

The natives of the Midi, France, were the first to wear middy skirts.

Before a man could become a monk he had to have his tonsils cut.

The government of Athens was democratic because the people made the laws with their own hands.

※

The government of England is a limited mockery.

※

The Constitution of the United States was adopted to secure domestic hostility.

※

Cyanide is so poisonous that one drop of it on a dog's tongue will kill the strongest man.

A horse divided against itself cannot stand.

※

Faith is that quality which enables us to believe what we know to be untrue.

The Bourbons were a French family that used to make
whisky.

A corps is a dead gentleman, a corpse is a dead lady.

A monologue is a conversation between two people,
such as husband and wife.

Moll Flanders is the story of a Belgian gun-girl.

※

Peter Minuit invented a very popular dance in the Colonial times.

※

Bisquit Tortoni was the man who discovered radio.

※

Iran is the bible of the Mohammedans.

※

Doctors now treat their patients with ultraviolent rays.

※

Chopin had many fast friends. Among the fastest was Miss Sand.

Hansom was a very good looking cab driver.

※

The chairman replied in a few appropriated words.

The mother of Abraham Lincoln died in infancy.

𝟙

Bach was the most famous composer in the world and
so was Handel.

𝟙

Paganini was a famous fiddler. He fiddled with many
of the greatest singers in Europe.

Solomon had 300 wives and 700 porcupines.

𝟙

Autobiography is a history of motor cars.

𝟙

A spa is a place where people go to drink their bath
water.

𝟙

Robinson Crusoe was a great operatic tenor.

Comic Dictionary

Acoustic An instrument used in shooting pool.

Acquaintance A person whom we know well enough to borrow from, but not well enough to lend to.

Ad Libber A man who stays up all night to memorize spontaneous jokes.

Adolescence The age between puberty and adultery.

Adult A person who has stopped growing at both ends and started growing in the middle.

Advertising A technique that makes you think you've longed all your life for something you've never heard of before.

After-Dinner Speaking The art of saying nothing briefly. An occupation monopolized by men . . . women can't wait that long!

Afternoon That part of the day spent figuring how we wasted the morning.

Alarm Clock A device for awakening childless households.

Alcohol   A liquid good for preserving almost anything except secrets.

Alimony   The high cost of leaving.

Ambassador An honest man sent abroad to lie for the commonwealth.

Americans   People who insist on living in the present tense.

Anatomy   Something everybody has—but it looks better on a girl.

Anecdote   A revealing account of an incident that never occurred in the life of some famous person.

Angel   A pedestrian who forgot to jump.

Ant   A small insect that, though always at work, still finds time to go to picnics.

August   The month you can't open the car window you couldn't close in February.

Baby   An alimentary canal with a loud voice at one end and no responsibility at the other.

Bachelor   A man who never makes the same mistake once.

Banjo   Let's not invite Joseph.

Bank   An institution where you can borrow money if you can present sufficient evidence to show that you don't need it.

Barber Shop   A clip joint.

Bargain   A transaction in which each party thinks he has cheated the other.

Basso Profundo   A deep-thinking fish.

Bath Mats   Little dry rugs that children like to stand beside.

Bathing Beauty   A girl who has a lovely profile all the way down.

Beach   A place where a girl goes in her baiting suit.

Beauty Contest   A lass roundup.

Bigamist   An Italian fog.

Bigamy   One wife too many. Monogamy is the same.

Boaster   A person who,. every time he opens his mouth, puts his feats in.

Bore   A guy with a cocktail glass in one hand, and your lapel in his other.

Boss of the Family   Whoever can spend ten dollars without thinking it necessary to say anything about it.

Brassiere   An invention designed to make a mountain out of a mole-hill, and vice versa.

Brat A kid that displays his pest manners.

Bridge A card game in which a good deal depends upon a good deal.

Bridge Expert One who can keep a kibitzer quiet all evening.

Broadway New York's main artery — the hardened artery.

Budget A mathematical confirmation of your suspicions.

Bureaucrat A man who shoots the bull, passes the buck, and makes seven copies of everything.

Bust Truster A man who is sure his girl doesn't wear falsies.

Busybody One who burns a scandal at both ends.

Caddy A lad who stands behind a golfer and didn't see the ball either.

Camelot A place where they park camels.

Carbuncle An auto collision.

Career Girl One who'd rather bring home the bacon than fry it.

Cauliflower A cabbage with a college education.

Chafing Dish   A pretty girl who has been stood up on a date.

Classic   A book which people praise and don't read.

Classical Music   The kind that we keep hoping will turn into a tune.

Coincide   What you do when it starts to rain.

Committee   A body that keeps minutes and wastes hours.

Community Chest   An organization that puts all its begs in one ask it.

Commuter   A traveling man who pays short visits to his home and office.

Conceit   A form of I-strain.

Conscience   A little gimmick inside you that makes

you tell your wife before somebody else does.

Conservative   One who believes that nothing should be done for the first time.

Consult   To seek another's approval of a course already decided upon.

Counter-Irritant   A woman who looks at everything and buys nothing.

Criminal   A person with predatory instincts who has not sufficient capital to form a corporation.

Crook   A business rival who has just left the room.

Cynic   One who knows the price of everything and the value of nothing.

Dachshund   Half a dog high and a dog and a half long.

Darkroom   A place where many a girl with a negative personality is developed.

Debate   It lures de fish.

Denial   A river in Egypt.

Dentist   A man who lives from hand to mouth.

Desk   A trash basket with drawers.

Detour   The roughest distance between two points.

Deuce   The unkindest cut of all.

Diner   A restaurant where you can eat dirt cheap . . . but who wants to eat dirt?'

Diplomacy   To do and say the nastiest things in the nicest way.

Diplomat   A fellow who has to watch his appease and accuse.

Dogma   A puppy's mother.

Economy   A way of spending money without getting any fun out of it.

Education   The knowledge that a chorus girl gets by stages and that a college girl gets by degrees.

Efficiency Expert   A guy smart enough to tell you how to run your business and too smart to start his own.

Egotist   A person of low taste, more interested in himself than me.

Elderly Wolf   One who's not gonna lust much longer.

Epigram   A wisecrack that has played Carnegie Hall.

Etiquette   Learning to yawn with your mouth closed.

Eunuch   One who is cut off from temptation.

Exchequer   A retired supermarket employee.

Expert   One who knows more and more about less and less.

Falsies   Hidden persuaders.

Firmness   That admirable quality in ourselves that is detestable stubborness in others.

Fish   The animal that seems to go for a vacation about the same time most fishermen do.

Flashlight   A case in which to carry dead batteries.

Forger   A man who gives a check a bad name.

Free Country One in which there is no particular individual to blame for the existing tyranny.

Gardening   A labor that begins with daybreak and ends with backbreak.

Genealogy   Tracing yourself back to people better than you are.

Genius   One who can do almost anything except make a living.

Gentleman   A worn-out wolf.

Girdle   A device to keep an unfortunate situation from spreading.

Gladiator   What the cannibal said after he ate the female explorer.

Gold-Digger   A girl with a gift of grab.

Golfer   A man who hits and tells.

Good-Bye   What money says when it talks.

Gossip   A woman with a nice sense of rumor.

Grade Crossing   The meeting place of headlights and light heads.

Grandmother   The person you bring the baby to for an overmauling.

Guest Towel   A small square of absorbent linen completely surrounded by useless embroidery.

Guillotine   A french chopping center.

Hangover   The wrath of grapes.

Happiness   A peculiar feeling you acquire when you're too busy to be miserable.

Heredity   Something you subscribe to whole-heartedly when your son's report card shows all A's.

Highbrow   A person who enjoys a thing until it becomes popular.

Hollywood   A place where you live happily and get married forever afterward.

Home   A place to go when all the other joints are closed.

Honest Politician   One who when he is bought will stay bought.

Horse-Sense   A degree of wisdom that keeps one from betting on the races.

Hospital Room   A place where friends of the patient go to talk to other friends of the patient.

Hospitals   Places where people who are run down wind up.

Hotel Guest   A person who leaves his room only because he can't get it into his bags.

Husband   What's left of a sweetheart after the nerve has been killed.

Hypothenuse	The washroom upstairs is occupied.
Igloo	An icicle built for two.
Indian Reservation	The home of the brave.
Inflation	Something that cost $10 to buy a few years ago and now costs $20 to repair.
Intoxication	To feel sophisticated and not be able to pronounce it.
Intuition	The instinct by which a woman can tell she's right whether she is or not.
Jacket Blurb	Fable of contents.
Jaywalking	An exercise that brings on that run-down feeling.
Jury	A group of 12 people selected to decide who has the better lawyer.
Kindergarten Teacher	One who should know how to make the little things count.
Knob	A thing to adore.
Lamb Stew	Much ado about mutton.
Las Vegas	The land of the spree and the home of the knave.
Linguist	One who has the ability to describe a beautiful girl without using his hands.

Litter The result of literary efforts.

Los Angeles Six suburbs in search of a city.

Madam For whom the belle toils.

Marriage An institution that starts with billing and cooing, but only the billing lasts.

Mayflower A small ship on which several million Pilgrims came to America in 1620.

Meteorologist A man who can look into a girl's eyes and tell whether.

Miniskirt Hemme fatale.

Minor Operation One performed on somebody else.

Mistress A cutie on the Q.T.

Molasses	Additional girls.
Money	Jack of all trades.
Monologue	A conversation between a real estate promoter and a prospect.
Mummy	An Egyptian who was pressed for time.
Neurotic	A person who has discovered the secret of perpetual emotion.
New Yorkers	A group of people who feel rich because they charge each other so much.
Night-Club Dancing	Merely lifting one's eyebrows in time to the music.
Nudist	A person who goes coatless and vestless, and wears trousers to match.
Oboe	An ill woodwind that nobody blows good.
Officer	A cop whom you can talk out of giving you a ticket.
Oily	The opposite of late.
Operator	An employee who takes the padding out of his shoulders and puts it in his expense account.
Out of Bounds	A pooped kangaroo.

Overeating   An activity which will make you thick to your stomach.

Pasteurize   Something you see moving.

Pedestrian   A chap who knows what the lady motorist is driving at.

Pessimist   A man who's always building dungeons in the air.

Petition   A list of people who didn't have the nerve to say no.

Petting   A study of anatomy in braille.

Pharmacist   Man in a white coat who stands behind a soda fountain and sells ballpoint pens.

Philosophical   The cheerful attitude assumed by everybody not directly involved in the trouble.

Platonic Lover   One who holds the eggshells while somebody else eats the omelette.

Polygon   A dead parrot.

Popular Girl   One who has been weighed in the ballance and found wanton.

Practical Nurse   One who marries a rich, elderly patient.

Procrastination   Putting off problems for a brainy day.

Procrastinator   Man with a wait problem.

Prune   A plum that has seen better days.

Psychology   The science that tells you what you already know in words you can't understand.

Public-Speaking   The art of diluting a two-minute idea with a two-hour vocabulary.

Punctuality   The art of guessing how late the other fellow is going to be.

Racehorse   An animal that can take several thousand people for a ride at the same time.

Radical   A conservative out of a job.

Ramshackle   A chain used to tie up a he-goat.

Regular Drinking Drinking between drinks.

Reno   The city of otherly love.

Repartee   An insult with its dress-suit on.

Resort   A place where the tired grow more tired.

Rummage Sale   A place where you can buy stuff from somebody else's attic to store in your own.

Sales Resistance The triumph of mind over patter.

Sex   The most fun you can have without laughing.

Shotgun Wedding A case of wife or death.

Silly Game One at which your wife can beat you.

Skeleton A man with his insides taken out and his outsides taken off.

Slang Language that takes off its coat, spits on its hands, and goes to work.

Small Fry A one-dollar steak.

Smart Cooky A girl who starts out with a little slip and ends up with a whole wardrobe.

Sneezing Much achoo about nothing.

Specimen An Italian astronaut.

Strength of Mind The ability to eat one salted peanut.

Sunbather A fry in the ointment.

Super Salesman One who can sell a double-breasted suit to a man with a Phi Beta Kappa key.

Swimming Pool A small body of water completely surrounded by other people's children.

Sympathy That which one woman offers another in exchange for the details.

Syntax	A levy on brothels.
Tact	The ability to make your guests feel at home when you wish they were.
Taxidermist	A man who knows his stuff.
Teutonic	Not enough gin.
Theory	A hunch with a college education.
Titian	The color a poor red-headed girl's hair becomes as soon as her father strikes oil.
Toothache	A pain that drives you to extraction.
Traffic Light	A little green light that changes to red as your car approaches.
Triangle	A figure invented by Euclid, tested by Don Juan, and brought to perfection by scenario writers.
Untouchables	People you can't borrow money from.
Used Car	A car in first crash condition.
Vacation	A period during which people find out where to stay away from next year.
Violin	A bad hotel.
Wallflower	A girl without a gent to her name.

Washington   The only place in the world where sound travels faster than light.

Wife   A person who can look in a bureau drawer and find the husband's tie clasp that isn't there.

Window Screen   A device for keeping flies in the house.

Wolf   A man who invites a girl for a scotch and sofa.

Yesmen   Fellows who hang around the man that nobody noes.

Cracks from the Critics

DOROTHY PARKER

The House Beautiful is the play lousy.

≋

ROBERT GARLAND

This show has to be seen to be depreciated.

≋

MONTY WOOLLEY

For the first time in my life I envied my feet. They were asleep.

≋

JOHN ANDERSON

The audience was so quiet, you could hear a pun drop.

≋

IRVING HOFFMAN

This show goes on my Best Smeller list.

≋

EUGENE FIELD

The actor who took the role of *King Lear* played the king as though he expected someone to play the ace.

≋

GROUCHO MARX

I saw the show under bad conditions—the curtain was up.

PERCY HAMMOND

I have knocked everything but the chorus girls' legs, and here God anticipated me.

※

FRANK NUGENT

A run of DeMille picture—March comes in like a lion and goes out like a ham.

J. NORMAN LYND

The quartet sang a derangement of an old favorite.

※

ALEXANDER WOOLLCOTT

The scenery was beautiful—but the actors got in front of it.

※

I just saw Isherwood's play *I Am a Camera.*
No Leica.

BROOKS ATKINSON

When Mr. Wilbur calls his play *Halfway to Hell*, he underestimates the distance.

ANONYMOUS

Last night the High School band played Beethoven. Beethoven lost.

※

ROBERT BENCHLEY

Perfectly Scandalous was one of those plays in which all of the actors unfortunately enunciated very clearly.

※

DOROTHY PARKER

Katherine Hepburn (in *The Lake*) runs the gamut of emotions from A to B.

Curses

In the Gay Nineties, curses were very fashionable and explicit. But in the cartoon strip, *Desperate Desmond*, where children's tender minds were to be protected, the villain could only grit his teeth and snarl at the hero, "Curses on you."

Here is a list of special beauties that we think you will find delicious—the crème de la crème of maledictions:

May you spend the best part of your day sitting on a soft chair . . . my dentist's.

May you be the proof that man can endure everything.

Break a leg and lose your crutch.

May you be a liar with a poor memory.

May you become so poor that you have to go around begging, and I hope you have to come to me for alms, and I hope I have nothing to give you.

Curses

Avoid old age . . . go hang yourself.

※

May you lose all your teeth except one—the one that
has the toothache.

※

Take a nice walk and stumble on a skunk.

※

May you grow like an onion—with your head in the
ground and your feet in the air.

May you romp with joy and skip right into a sewer.

May all your relatives move in on you.

※

May student barbers practice on your beard.

※

May all your baths be too hot and your women too cold.

※

May everything you cook stick to the bottom of the pot.

※

May you become famous—in medical history.

May your wife eat matzohs in bed, and may you roll in the crumbs.

Curses

May all your shoes be too long and your haircuts too short.

May you spend your healthy days on your back, your sick days on your feet.

May your hat be the right size, but your head too small.

May your appetite enlarge and your digestion diminish.

May your wife be as much help to you as a lame horse.

May you bargain with God and lose.

May you turn out like a lamp, to hang all day and burn all night.

Go eat apples—and bite into worms.

Funeral Notices

Little Alexander's dead;
    Jam him in a coffin;
Don't have as good a chance
    For a fun'ral often.
Rush his body right around
    To the cemetery;
Drop him in the sepulchre
    With his Uncle Jerry.

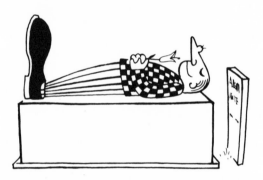

The death-angel smote Alexander McGlue,
    And gave him protracted repose;
He wore a checked shirt and a number twelve shoe,
    And he had a huge wart on his nose.
No doubt he is happier dwelling in space
    Over there on the evergreen shore.
His friends are informed that his funeral takes place
    Precisely at quarter-past four.

She was such a little seraph that her father, who is
  sheriff,
Really doesn't seem to care if he ne'er smiles in
  life again.
She has gone, we hope, to heaven, at the early age
  of seven
(Funeral starts off at eleven), where she'll nevermore have pain.

※

Oh! bury Bartholomew out in the woods,
  In a beautiful hole in the ground,
Where the bumble-bees buzz and the woodpeckers sing,
  And the straddle-bugs tumble around;
So that, in winter, when the snow and the slush
  Have covered his last little bed,
His brother Artemas can go out with Jane
  And visit the place with his sled.

※

Four doctors tackled Johnny Smith—
  They blistered and they bled him;
With squills and anti-bilious pills
  And ipecac, they fed him.

They stirred him up with calomel,
  And tried to move his liver;
But all in vain—his little soul
  Was wafted o'er The River.

Funny Ads

For sale ad in the Los Angeles Times:
BLACK BEAR RUG. North American. Fur excellent condition. Was a movie star.

※

Personal in the La Marque, Texas Times:
Unemployed diamonds for sale at big discount. New four-diamond wedding ring. Slightly used seven-diamond engagement ring. Bought in burst of enthusiasm for $550, sentimental value gone, will sacrifice for $250.

※

From a Long Island paper:
For Sale—Large crystal vase by lady slightly cracked.

※

For sale ad in the Bayside, N.Y. Selling Post:
Pair Adjustable Crutches, used one month, $5; Roof Shingles, new, $2 bundle.

※

From the Long Beach, Cal. Tri-Shopper:
Jointer-Plane—used once to cut off thumb. Will sell cheap.

Funny Ads

From the Grand Rapids Press:
Gelding—spirited but gentle. Ideal for teen-ager. For sale by parents whose daughter has discovered boys are more interesting than horses.

※

Personal in a New York paper:
Young man who gets paid on Monday and is broke by Wednesday would like to exchange small loans with a young man who gets paid on Wednesday and is broke by Monday.

※

From a classified ad in a Boone, Iowa paper:
Wanted—To trade saxophone in fancy case for fresh cow.

In the personal columns of a rural weekly:
Anyone found near my chicken house at night will be found there next morning.

From the Clifton Forge, Va. Daily Review:
Save regularly in our bank. You'll never reget it.

※

In the merchandise columns of the Philadelphia Inquirer:
Tombstone slightly used. Sell cheap. Weil's Curiosity Shop.

※

Personal in the Greenwich Village, N.Y. Village Voice:
At Last! After years of intensive study for the concert stage, I am now prepared to offer my services as an accomplished male baby-sitter.

※

In Shears, the journal of the box-making industry:
Situation Wanted—by young woman 21 years of age. Unusual experience includes three years Necking and Stripping. Address Dept. 0-2, Shears.

※

From a Missouri paper:
Wanted—Men, women and children to sit in slightly used pews on Sunday morning.

※

From the Sumner, Ia. Gazette:
Wanted—To trade guitar for shotgun.

Classified ad in the New York Herald Tribune:
Man wanted to work in dynamite factory; must be willing to travel.

❀

From the Atlanta Journal:
Wanted—A mahogany living room table, by a lady with Heppelwhite legs.

❀

From an Indianapolis paper:
Have you lost track of your creditors? Let us locate them.

❀

From a Parsons, Pa. paper:
Easter Matinee—Saturday Morning 10:30 a.m. Every child laying an egg in the door man's hand will be admitted free.

From the Hartford Times:
Front room, suitable for two laddies, use of kitchen or two gentlemen.

☀

From the Paris Herald:
Buy your fancy necklaces directly from the manufacturer—100 per cent cheaper.

☀

From a Baltimore paper:
Big cattle show at Tolchester Beach. Go over, see the show and meet your friends.

☀

From a Jamesville, Iowa paper:
Get rid of aunts. T—does job in 24 hours. 25¢ per bottle.

☀

From a Chatham, Ontario paper:
Special foul dinner, 45¢.

☀

From an El Paso paper:
Widows made to order. Send us your specifications.

☀

From a New York paper:
Sheer stockings—Designed for dressy wear, but so serviceable that lots of women wear nothing else.

Funny Ads

From a Montesan, Wash. paper:

For sale—A full blooded cow, giving three gallons milk, two tons of hay, a lot of chickens and a cookstove.

✻

From a Willimantic, Conn. paper:

Wanted—A strong horse to do the work of a country minister.

From a Jacksonville paper:

Man, honest, will take anything.

✻

From the San Antonio Light:

Grocery and meat market with loving rooms; no competition, a bargain quick sale; leaving town.

From the Birmingham Age-Herald:
Wanted—Farm mule. Must be reasonable.

※

From The New York Times:
Situation wanted—Houseworker, plain crook, reliable.

※

From the Abilene, Tex. Reporter-News:
$10 reward for south side apartment. Large enough to keep young wife from going home to mother. Small enough to keep mother from coming here.

※

From a department-store ad in the Elmira, N.Y. Star-Gazette:
Whatever type your father is, we know we can help you choose a gift to make him grim all over.

※

From a New Jersey paper:
Visit our clothing department. We can outwit the whole family.

※

From a Burns, Oregon paper:
Why go elsewhere to be cheated when you can come here?

Funny Ads

From a Los Angeles paper:

The factory stands back of each fruit juice extractor against all defects, for one year. Truly it is a germ.

We have found it impossible to locate the source of the following gems.

Will the mother whose little boy laid his half-sucked lollipop on a mahogany end table please come in again? She can have the end table for exactly one dollar, with the lollipop still intact.

✻

Attractive kitten seeks position purring in a nice little girl's lap. Will also do light mouse work.

✻

Will the lady who saved $90 on electric washer I advertised in last week's *Gazette* please get in

91

touch with me? It was the drier my wife wanted to sell.

※

Will the party who picked up the black cocker spaniel puppy Friday on the boardwalk either return him or come back and get the heartbroken four-year-old boy he belongs to?

※

For sale—Diamonds: $3; microscopes: $2.75.

※

Wanted—Smart young lady to act as deceptionist.

※

For sale—38-foot cruiser. A beauty equipped with two bailing pumps. May be seen by appointment. Bring diving helmet.

※

Send for a box of our homemade soap. It doesn't lather. It doesn't float. It contains no secret ingredients. It is designed solely to keep you company in the tub.

※

Dinner Special—Turkey $1.35; Chicken or Beef $1.25; Children $1.00.

Funny Epitaphs

In Hatfield, Mass.:
>Beneath this stone, a lump of clay, lies Arabella
>   Young;
>Who on the 21st of May began to hold her tongue.

※

Over the grave of a dentist:
>Stranger! Approach this spot with gravity!
>John Brown is filling his last cavity.

※

In an English cemetery:
>It was a cough that carried him off,
>It was a coffin they carried him off in.

※

In Lost Creek, Colorado:
>Here lies the clay of Mitchel Coots,
>Whose feet yet occupy his boots.
>His soul has gone—we know not where
>It landed, neither do we care.
>He slipped a joker up his sleeve
>With vile intention to deceive;
>And when detected, tried to jerk
>His gun, but didn't get his work
>In with sufficient swiftness, which
>Explains the presence here of Mitch.

In Falkirk, England:
>At rest beneath this slab of stone,
>   Lies stingy Jimmy Wyett;
>He died one morning just at ten
>   And saved a dinner by it!

※

On the grave of his wife:
>Here lies my wife: here let her lie!
>Now she's at rest—and so am I.

John Dryden

※

In St. Mary Winston College, Oxford, over Merideth, an organist:
>Here lies one blown out of breath,
>Who lived a merry life, and died a Merideth.

※

Epitaph for a friend:
>On the twenty-second of June
>Jonathan Fiddle went out of tune.

Ben Jonson

※

In Oxfordshire, England:
>Here lies the body of John Eldred
>At least, he will be when he's dead;
>But now at this time he's alive
>The 14th of August, Sixty-five.

Funny Epitaphs

In St. George's Churchyard, Somerset·
Here lies Poor Charlotte,
Who died no harlot,
But in her virginity,
Though just turned nineteen
Which within this vicinty
Is hard to be found and seen.

In Enosburg, Vermont:
Here lies the body of our Anna
Done to death by a banana;
It wasn't the fruit that laid her low,
But the skin of the thing that made her go!

※

In the Cheltenham Churchyard:
Here lie I and my two daughters,
Killed by drinking Cheltenham waters.
If we had stuck to Epsom Salts
We wouldn't be lying in these vaults.

On the tombstone of a pedestrian:
    This is the grave of Mike O'Day
    Who died maintaining his right of way.
    His right was clear, his will was strong,
    But he's just as dead as if he'd been wrong.

In Boot Hill Cemetery, Dodge City, Kansas:
    Played five aces.
    Now playing the harp.

At Great Torrington, Devon:
    Here lies a man who was killed by lightning;
    He died when his prospects seemed to be
        brightening,
    He might have cut a flash in this world of trouble,
    But the flash cut him, and he lies in the stubble.

Funny Epitaphs

On the grave of a fisherman:
Here lies the body of Jonathan Stout,
He fell in the water and never got out,
And still is supposed to be floating about.

※

In Pawtucket, R.I. over Dr. William Rothwell, who always paid the check at parties:
This is on me.

※

In Pere Làchaise Cemetery, Paris:
Here lies Pierre Cobachard, grocer.
His inconsolable widow dedicates this monument to his memory, and continues the same business at the old stand, 167 Rue Mouffetard.

※

In Suffolk, England:
Stranger pass by and waste no time
On bad biography and careless rhyme.
For what I am, this humble dust encloses;
And what I was is no affair of yourses.

※

In Falkirk, England:
Here under this sod and under these trees
Is buried the body of Solomon Pease,
But here in this hole lies only his pod
His soul is shelled out and gone to God.

At Selby, Yorkshire:
Here lies my wife, a sad slattern and shrew;
If I said I regretted her, I should lie too!

On the tombstone of an orator:
Here lies the body of Cynthia Near
Whose mouth it stretched from ear to ear.
Tread softly, stranger, o'er this wonder,
For if she yawns, you're gone by thunder!

In Bath Abbey:
Here lies Ann Mann; she lived an old
Maid and she died an old *Mann.*

In Burlington, Mass.:
Here lies the body of Susan Lowder
Who burst while drinking Seidlitz powder;
Called from this world to her Heavenly rest—
She should have waited till it effervesced!

Funny Epitaphs

In Medway, Mass.:
> Beneath this stone, a lump of clay,
> Lies Uncle Peter Daniels,
> Who too early in the month of May
> Took off his winter flannels!

✲

On the grave of a waiter:
> By and by
> God caught his eye.

✲

In Brookfield, Conn.:
> My wife lies here.
> I am glad of it.

✲

At Fosbrooke, in Northumberland:
> Here lieth Matthew Hollingshead,
> Who died from cold caught in his head.
> It brought on fever and rheumatiz,
> Which ended me—for here I is!

✲

In Boot Hill Cemetery, Kansas:
> Shoot-'em-up Jake—
> Ran for sheriff, 1872;
> Ran from sheriff, 1876;
> Buried, 1876.

In Shutesbury, Mass.:
> Here lies my husbands, I, II, III,
> Dumb as men could ever be.
> As for my IV'th, well, praise be God!
> He bides for a little above the sod.
> Alex, Ben, Sandy were the first three's names,
> And to make things tidy, I'll add his—James.

※

In Hollis, N.H.:
> Here lies Cynthia, Stevens' wife,
> She lived six years in calm and strife.
> Death came at last and set her free,
> I was glad and so was she.

※

In Winslow, Maine:
> Here Betsy Brown her body lies,
> Her soul is flying to the skies.
> While here on earth she oft-times spun
> Six hundred skeins from sun to sun,
> And wove one day, her daughter brags,
> Two hundred pounds of carpet rags.

※

In Canaan, N.H.:
> He heard the angels calling him
>> From the Celestial Shore,
> He flapped his wings and away he went
>> To make one angel more.

In Sargentville, Maine:
>Beneath these stones do lie,
>Back to back, my wife and I!
>When the last trumpet the air shall fill,
>If she gets up, I'll just lie still.

❋

In Bunhill Fields Burying Ground, England:
>In 67 months she was tapped 66 times. Had taken away 240 gallons of water, without ever repining at her case, or even feating the operation.

In Canaan, New Hampshire:
>Here lies, cut down like unripe fruit,
>The wife of Deacon Amos Shute.
>She died of drinking too much coffee,
>Anno Dominy eighteen forty.

In Skaneateles, New York:
Underneath this pile of stones
Lies all that's left of Sally Jones.
Her name was Briggs; it was not Jones,
But Jones was used to rhyme with stones!

❦

In Providence, R.I.:
The wedding day decided was,
The wedding wine provided,
But ere the day did come along
He'd drunk it and died, did.
Ah, Sidney! Sidney!

❦

On Charles II:
Here lies our sovereign lord the king,
   Whose word no man relies on;
He never says a foolish thing,
   Nor ever does a wise one.

Lord Rochester

❦

In Plymouth, Mass.:
Here lies the bones of Richard Lawton,
Whose death, alas! was strangely brought on.
Trying his corns one day to mow off,
His razor slipped and cut his toe off.
His toe, or, rather, what it grew to,
An inflamation quickly flew to.
Which took, alas! to mortifying
And was the cause of Richard's dying.

In Burlington, Vt.:
>Beneath this stone our baby lays,
>He neither cries nor hollers,
>He lived just one and twenty days,
>And cost us forty dollars.

※

In Kilmurry Churchyard, Ireland:
>This stone was raised by Sarah's lord,
>Not Sarah's virtues to record—
>For they're well known to all the town—
>But it was *raised* to keep her *down*.

※

In Skaneateles, N.Y.:
>Neuralgia worked on Mrs. Smith
>Till neath the sod it laid her.
>She was a worthy Methodist
>And served as a crusader.

※

In Williamsport, Pa., over the grave of a man kicked to death by a colt:
>Peaceable and quiet, a friend to his father and mother, and respected by all who knew him, and went to the world where horses do not kick, where sorrow and weeping is no more.

In Lee, Mass.:

> Open wide ye heavenly gates
> That lead to the heavenly shore;
> Our father suffered in passing through
> And mother weighs much more.

※

In Lincoln, Maine:

> SACRED TO THE MEMORY OF JARED BATES
> WHO DIED AUG. THE 6TH, 1800
>
> His Widow, aged 24, lives at 7 Elm Street,
> has every qualification for a good wife, and
> yearns to be comforted.

※

In Hadley Churchyard, England:

> The charnal mounted on the w-
> Sets to be seen in funer-
> A matron plain, domestic-
> In care and pain continu-
> Not slow, not gay, nor prodig-
> Yet neighborly, and hospit-   } ALL
> Her children seven yet living
> Her sixty-seventh year hence did c-
> To rest her body natur-
> In hopes to rise spiritu-

Funny Epitaphs

From an English village cemetery:
Here lies a miser who lived for himself,
And cared for nothing but gathering pelf,
Now where he is or how he fares,
Nobody knows and nobody cares.

※

In a 17th-century English churchyard:
Here lies the body of Ethan Bevan,
Killed by lightning sent from heaven
For trading horses on Sunday, June eleven,
In the year Eighteen Hundred Twenty-seven.

※

And here are a few final inscriptions—fictitious, of course—that might fittingly adorn the gravestones of some famous personalities.

Clive Brook:
Excuse me for not rising.

Lionel Barrymore:
Well, I've played everything but a harp.

Walter Winchell:
Here lies Walter Winchell in the dirt he loved so well.

Ilka Chase:
I've finally gotten to the bottom of things.

Dorothy Parker:
Involved in a plot.

Hilarious Headlines

From a Heraldsburg, Cal. paper:
CAR LEAVES ROAD, SUFFERS BROKEN NOSE

⁂

From a Burlingame, Cal. paper:
SANTA ROSA MAN DENIES HE COMMITTED SUICIDE
IN SAN FRANCISCO

⁂

From the Spokane Chronicle:
GRILL SUSPECT OVER BIG BLAZE

⁂

From the Boise, Idaho Statesman, announcing birth of
triplets:
THREE OF A KIND GIVES PAIR FULL HOUSE

⁂

From an Oakland, Cal. paper:
HAMM FAILS TO IDENTIFY YEGGS

⁂

From a Dallas paper:
THUGS EAT THEN ROB PROPIETOR

From the Toledo Times:

SCENT FOUL PLAY IN DEATH OF MAN FOUND BOUND AND HANGED

From a San Francisco paper:

DEAD OFFICER ON S.F. FORCE FOR 18 YEARS

From the Halifax, Canada Herald:

JUNE BABIES FLOOD OTTAWA HOSPITAL

From a New York paper, reporting on a rape by a group of soldiers:

COMMISSION TO EXAMINE PRIVATES—WILL LEAVE NO STONE UNTURNED

From the San Antonio, Tex. Express:

"LEONORE" ONLY OPERA BEETHOVEN WROTE ON MONDAY EVENING

From an Oshkosh, Wis. paper:
PEACE OR WAR DEEMED NEAR

※

From the La Grange, Ga. News:
REV. KEY RESIGNS; ATTENDANCE DOUBLES

※

From the Wheeling, W. Va. Intelligencer:
WILD WIFE LEAGUE WILL MEET TO-NIGHT

From a Walla Walla, Wash. paper:
ONION PROSPECTS REPORTED STRONG

※

From the Springfield Republican:
40 MEN ESCAPE WATERY GRAVES WHEN VESSEL
FLOUNDERS IN ALE

From a Los Angeles paper:
COUNTY OFFICIALS TO TALK RUBBISH

❄

From the Greensboro, N.C. News:
SAM M–, 80, HELD FOR SHOOTING GRANDMOTHER'S
HUSBAND

❄

From the Chicago Tribune:
WIFE GIVES BIRTH TO A BOY; HE ASKS OLD AGE
PENSION

❄

From the Boston Transcript:
HOTEL BURNS; TWO HUNDRED GUESTS ESCAPE HALF
GLAD

❄

From a Bridgeport, Conn. paper:
INFANT MORALITY SHOWS DROP HERE

❄

From the Lansing State Journal:
SENATE PASSES DEATH PENALTY—Measure Provides
for Electrocution for All Persons Over 17.

❄

From a New York paper:
FATHER OF TEN SHOT—MISTAKEN FOR
RABBIT

From the Wichita Falls, Tex. Record News:
ENRAGED COW INJURES FARMER WITH AX

From the Oakland, Cal. Tribune:
TWO CONVICTS EVADE NOOSE; JURY HUNG

※

From the New York Journal-American:
STEALS CLOCK, FACES TIME

※

From an Austin, Tex. paper:
JURY GETS DRUNK DRIVING CASE HERE

※

From a Texas paper:
NEBRASKA OFFICERS BEST BANK
BANDITS

From the Cleveland Plain Dealer:
GYPSY ROSE HAS A 5½-POUND STRIPLING

※

From an Alhambra, Cal. paper:
DRIVER OF DEATH CAR HELD ON NEGLIGIBLE HOMICIDE

※

From a Los Cruces, N.M. paper:
MAN IS FATALLY SLAIN

From the Redondo Beach, Cal. South Bay Daily Breeze:
MANY ANTIQUES AT D.A.R. MEETING

How's Business?

Here are some likely responses to the above question by various tradesmen.

SAID THE SAILOR:	*Knot bad.*
SAID THE COFFEE SALESMAN:	*It's a grind.*
SAID THE DRUMMER:	*It's hard to beat.*

SAID THE ASTRONOMER:	*Things are looking up.*
SAID THE DRESSMAKER:	*Just sew-sew.*
SAID THE DEMOLITION WORKER:	*Smashing!*
SAID THE STREETCLEANER:	*Things are picking up.*

How's Business?

SAID THE PIANIST:	*Right on key.*
SAID THE BULLFIGHTER:	*In the red.*
SAID THE GUNSMITH:	*Booming!*
SAID THE BOTANIST:	*Everything's coming up roses.*

SAID THE BARTENDER:	*It's been pretty tight lately.*
SAID THE LOCKSMITH:	*Everything's opening up.*
SAID THE SEWER WORKER:	*I've been getting to the bottom of things.*
SAID THE MUSICIAN:	*Nothing of note has been happening.*

SAID THE COUNTERMAN: *Pretty crummy.*

SAID THE COUNTERFEITER: *We're forging on.*

SAID THE ICEMAN: *Not so hot.*

SAID THE GRAVEDIGGER: *Monumental!*

SAID THE TEACHER: *My work is classy.*

SAID THE ZOO KEEPER: *It's beastly!*

SAID THE FLOOR WAXER: *Going smoothly.*

SAID THE DAIRY FARMER: *Cheesy, in a whey.*

SAID THE TOBACCONIST: *It's a drag.*

SAID THE BAKER: *I've been making a. lot of dough lately.*

SAID THE TREE SURGEON: *I've some shady deals going.*

SAID THE PILOT: *Pretty much up in the air.*

SAID THE PHOTOGRAPHER: *Everything is clicking—and developing well.*

SAID THE DEEP-SEA DIVER: *I'm about to go under.*

Humorous Signs

In a New York restaurant:
Customers who consider our waitresses uncivil ought to see the manager.

※

In the window of a Kentucky dealer in washing machines:
Don't kill your wife. Let our washing machines do the dirty work.

On a New York loft building:
Wanted—Woman to sew buttons on the fourth floor.

※

In a Chicago restaurant:
Dreaded Veal Cutlets

In a restaurant in Cleveland, Ohio, which featured a 50-cent hang-over breakfast:
> One jumbo orange juice, toast, coffee, two aspirins and our sympathy.

In Pennsylvania, surmounted on a large reproduction of a match:
> This is the forest prime evil.

In a brassiere shoppe:
> We fix Flats.

On the card of a Hollywood jewelry store:
> We hire out wedding rings.

On a Tennessee highway:
> Take Notice: When this sign is under water, this road is impassable.

Above the coffee percolator of a roadside dining car east of Lancaster, Pa.:

Use less sugar and stir like the devil. We don't mind the noise.

※

On a blackboard outside a London church, during the blitz:

If your knees are knocking, kneel on them.

※

In an Arkansas shoe repair shop:

If your shoes aren't ready, don't blame us. Two of our employees have gone after a heel to save your soles.

※

On a Connecticut road:

Drive like hell, and you'll get there.

※

In a Montreal restaurant:

The Early Bird Gets the Worm! Special Shoppers' Luncheon before 11 a.m.

※

In a cemetery at South Bethlehem, Pa.:

Persons are prohibited from picking flowers from any but their own graves.

In a General Motors plant:
According to the theory of aerodynamics and as may be readily demonstrated through wind tunnel experiments, the bumblebee is unable to fly. This is because the size, weight and shape of his body in relation to the total wing-spread make flying impossible. BUT THE BUMBLEBEE, BEING IGNORANT OF THESE SCIENTIFIC TRUTHS, GOES AHEAD AND FLIES ANYWAY—AND MAKES A LITTLE HONEY EVERY DAY.

※

In the Jackson Park Hospital Obstetrical Ward:
No Children Allowed.

※

In an Oslo store window:
English Spoken, American Understood.

※

On a farm-gate in Ohio:
Peddlers beware! We shoot every tenth peddler. The ninth one just left.

In a New York restaurant:
Pies like mother used to make before she took to bridge and cigarettes.

❉

In a Seattle butcher shop:
Pork sausages from pigs that died happy.

❉

On a Jamestown, N.Y. movie marquee:
ONE RECKLESS MOMENT

BABY MAKES THREE

❉

Placard hanging in the office of the Farrell Lines steamship company:
THINK—or thwim.

❉

Metal plaque on the crest of California's 12-million-ton Shasta Dam:
U.S. government property. Do not remove.

❉

On a Kentucky farm:

NOTIS

Trespassers will be persecuted to the full extent of two mongrel dogs which ain't never been too sociable with strangers and one dubble barrel shotgun which ain't loaded with sofa pillows. Dam if I ain't gittin tired to this hell raisin round my place.

※

In a West Coast dance hall:
The management reserves the right to exclude any lady they think proper.

※

In a Delaware chemical plant:
If you insist on smoking, please tell us where to send the ashes.

※

In a Miami Beach restaurant:
If you are over eighty years old and accompanied by your parents, we will cash your check.

※

In the maternity department of a St. Louis hospital:
Ladies Ready to Bear Department.

※

On a movie theatre:
Children's Matinee Today. Adults Not Admitted Unless With Child.

※

On a Los Angeles dance hall:
Good Clean Dancing Every Night but Sunday.

On a Los Angeles body-and-fender repair shop:
  May We Have the Next Dents?

※

Menu in a Chicago restaurant:
  Barely Soup.

※

In a college book store:
  Help fight TV. Buy a book!

※

In a toy department:
  Five Santa Clauses. No waiting.

Warning posted in an office at a southern air base:
  CAUTION—Make sure brain is engaged before putting mouth into gear.

In a garage in Albuquerque, N.M.:
Don't smoke around the gasoline tank. If your life isn't worth anything, gasoline is!

From a Newport newspaper:
Swim at the new pool—With suits, 35¢. Without suits, 50¢.

❉

In the lobby of a hotel in Rochester, Minn., home of the Mayo Clinic:
Please do not discuss your operation in the lobby.

❉

In a restaurant near an Army camp:
Watch your coat, hat, and girl friend.

❉

On a Los Angeles movie marquee:
GO FOR BROKE
LAS VEGAS STORY

In front of an Oshkosh mortuary chapel:
The fact that those we have served once return again, and recommend us to their friends, is a high endorsement of the service we render.

※

Outside London striptease theatre:
HERE THE BELLES PEEL

※

On a newly seeded lawn at Wellesley College:
Don't Ruin the Gay Young Blades!

Flashed on the screen of an Albany, N.Y. motion picture theatre:
A $5.00 bill has been found in the aisle. Will the owner please form a line outside the box-office.

In a Florida cocktail lounge:
Please don't stand up while the room is in motion.

In a yard near Lake Arrowhead, Cal.:
Worms with Fish Appeal.

Across a blasted wine shop window in Birmingham, England:
We are carrying on with unbroken spirits.

In a Tacoma men's clothing store window:
FIFTEEN MEN'S WOOL SUITS—$3.00
They won't last an hour!

On a dairy:
You can't beat our milk, but you can whip our cream.

Billboard near North Augusta, S.C.:
Try Our Easy Payment Plan. 100% Down. No
Future Worries About Payment.

※

On Bing Crosby's front lawn:
Keep off the grass. Remember when you, too, were
struggling for recognition.

※

On a barbecue stand that had gone out of business:
Opened By Mistake!

※

In a Pittsburgh bakery window:
CREAM PUFFS—6 FOR 29¢
The flakiest, puffiest of puffs crammed full of
creamy mustard.

※

In a Kingston, Ont. repair shop:
Closed July 1 to July 15.
Open July 21 for sure.

※

In clinic waiting room:
Ladies in the Waiting Room will Please Not Ex-
change Symptoms. It gets the Doctors Hopelessly
Confused.

In a Rochester plumber's window:
    Do it yourself—then call us before it's too late.

※

In a Shreveport realtor's window:
    Get lots while you're young.

※

On a church bulletin board:
    This church is prayer-conditioned.

In the window of a Boston necktie emporium:
    Come in and tie one on.

On a convalescent home in New York:
For the sick and tired of the Episcopal Church.

❋

Name of a Hollywood restaurant:
EATER'S DIGEST

In a Bronx window:
Piano lessons; special pains given to beginners.

❋

Outside a Westwood, Cal. restaurant:
We have no idea where Mom is, but we've got Pop on ice.

❋

On a divorce lawyer's wall:
Satisfaction guaranteed or your honey back.

In a New York factory:
Any workman desiring to attend the funeral of a near relative must notify the foreman before ten A.M. on the day of the game.

❊

On the license plate of a hearse in Norwich, Conn.:
U-2.

❊

On a delicatessen store wall:
Our Best Is None Too Good.

❊

On a peanut stand:
If our peanuts were any fresher, they'd be insulting.

❊

At a New Jersey intersection:
Cross Road—Better Humor It!

❊

In a butcher shop window during a meat shortage:
LEG O'NUTTIN

❊

On the ashtrays in the judge's library of the U.S. Circuit Court of Appeals in New York:
Not Government property. Please do not take from library.

Irish Bulls

An Irish bull is a grotesque blunder in language, differing from a malapropism in that the blunder lies not in the misuse of words, but in a complete confusion of ideas—which usually results in a joining of two mutually exclusive concepts. Webster defines an Irish bull as "an expression containing apparent congruity but actual incongruity of ideas," and gives us this almost perfect example: "He remarked in all seriousness that it was hereditary in his family to have no children."

The Irish bulls that follow could easily challenge Webster's best.

"Dear Molly," wrote O'Neill, "this is the fourth letter I've written to you asking for your hand in marriage. If you still refuse, please return this letter unopened."

※

"Begorra, Willie," Mike exclaimed as he finished a final pint and rose unsteadily to his feet, "but I haven't the faintest notion where I left my cap. Have you seen it?"

"I have," replied Willie. "It's on your head."

"Indeed it is! And it's a good thing you found it, or I'd have gone off without it."

"Mercy me!" Mrs. Murphy said to her husband, "but wasn't that a terrible thunder and lighting storm we had last night."

"You don't say!" replied Murphy. "Why didn't you wake me? You know I can't sleep when it thunders like that!"

※

"Why do Irishmen always enjoy a brawl?" asked the American tourist.

"That's simple," replied O'Leary. "An Irishman is never at peace except when he's fighting."

"Your money or your life!" cried the stick-up man, brandishing a revolver.

"Take my life," replied Casey, "I'm saving my money for my old age."

"An Irishman," noted Flynn, "will die before he'd let himself be buried in any but an Irish cemetery."

"Callahan!" cried Hogan, after his friend had tripped and fallen into the gutter. "Are you all right?"

"I can't answer you," replied Callahan, "I've been knocked speechless."

※

"Abstinence is a fine thing," observed Paddy. "But it must always be practiced in moderation."

※

"You're such a pest," the father scolded his misbehaving child. "The next time I take you out I'll leave you home."

Letter-Perfect

It's really not that tough to construct a sentence which employs every letter of the alphabet at least once. The trick comes in when you try to keep the *total* number of letters in the sentence down to a bare minimum. A letter-perfect sentence of this sort would, naturally, employ 26 letters—no more, no less. Take a look at these near misses.

A QUICK BROWN FOX JUMPS OVER THE LAZY DOG.
(33 letters)

PACK MY BOX WITH FIVE DOZEN LIQUOR JUGS.
(32 letters)

QUICK WAFTING ZEPHYRS VEX BOLD JIM.
(29 letters)

And here's the best one we've ever seen, employing only 28 letters. (If you come up with a more economical sentence of this kind, let us know *immediately*.)

WALTZ, NYMPH,
FOR QUICK JIGS VEX BUD.

Limericks

The limerick is now an abiding part of our literature. A highly disciplined verse form, compact and clever, it tells a story in only five lines. Unlike most basic forms of English verse, such as the sonnet and the triolet, the limerick was not borrowed from other countries but is indigenously English, perhaps the only form in poetry that can be claimed to be an original English creation.

Undoubtedly, the limerick is the most quoted of all verse forms extant today. From the drawing room to the classroom, whether recited in a surreptitious whisper or blared forth uproariously, the limerick has captivated almost every echelon of society. Popular everywhere, it has especially become the darling of the intellectual.

The limerick reflects the temper of its day. Additions to this great fund of versification have been made by outstanding poets and publicists. Some of the most widely recited limericks have been ascribed, perhaps apocryphally, to Alfred Lord Tennyson, Norman Douglas, Eugene Field, Don Marquis, Heywood Broun, Woodrow Wilson, among others.

Back in the 1860's Edward Lear penned these rhythmical five-line ditties for children. But the form soon bounded out of the nursery onto the campus; and from there into the market place, the counting house, and the army. Once out on the streets and in full contact with the foibles, frustrations, and fantasies of the common folk, the limerick began to reflect the thoughts of the people more and more plain-spokenly. The more pungent, punchy, and bawdy, the more easily were these verses remembered, and the more frequently were they quoted.

The limerick packs laughs anatomical
Into space that is quite economical.
But the good ones I've seen
So seldom are clean
And the clean ones so seldom are comical.

There was a young lady named Banker,
Who slept while the ship lay at anchor;
She awoke in dismay
When she heard the mate say:
"Now hoist up the topsheet, and spanker!"

The limerick, peculiar to English,
Is a verse form that's hard to extinguish.
    Once Congress in session
    Decreed its suppression
But people got around it by writing the last
    line without any rhyme or meter.

⁂

There was a young lady named Bright,
Who traveled much faster than light.
    She started one day
    In the relative way,
And returned on the previous night.

⁂

A man to whom illness was chronic,
When told that he needed a tonic,
    Said, "Oh, Doctor, dear,
    Won't you please make it beer?"
"No, no," said the Doc, "that's Teutonic."

⁂

There was a young maid from Madras,
Who had a magnificent ass;
    Not rounded and pink,
    As you probably think—
It was gray, had long ears, and ate grass.

There was an old party of Lyme,
Who lived with three wives at one time.
　When asked, "Why the third?"
　He replied, "One's absurd,
And bigamy, sir, is a crime!"

※

Another young poet in China
Had a feeling for rhythm much fina.
　His limericks tend
　To come to an end
Quite suddenly.

There was a young lady named Maud,
A very deceptive young fraud;
　She never was able
　To eat at the table,
But out in the pantry—*O Lord!*

Said the chemist: "I'll take some dimethyloximidomeso-
    ralamide
And I'll add just a dash of dimethylamidoazobensalde-
    hyde;
    But if these won't mix,
    I'll just have to fix
Up a big dose of trisodiumpholoroglucintricarboxycide.

※

God's plan made a hopeful beginning
But man spoiled his chances by sinning.
    We trust that the story
    Will end in God's glory—
But at present the other side's winning.

※

There was a young fellow named Wier,
Who hadn't an atom of fear.
    He indulged a desire
    To touch a live wire.
(Most any last line will do here!)

※

There's a wonderful family, called Stein,
There's Gert and there's Epp and there's Ein;
    Gert's poems are bunk,
    Epp's statues are junk,
And no one can understand Ein.

As a beauty I am not a star,
There are others more handsome by far;
   But my face—I don't mind it,
   Because I'm behind it;
It's the people in front that I jar.

Anthony Euwer

※

There was a young man of Japan
Whose limericks never would scan.
   When someone asked why
   He replied with a sigh,
"It's because I always try to get as many words
   into the last line as I possibly can."

※

I wish that my room had a floor
I don't so much care for a door,
   But this walking around
   Without touching the ground
Is getting to be quite a bore!

※

There was an Old Man of St. Bees
Who was stung in the arm by a wasp.
   When asked, "Does it hurt?"
   He replied, "No, it doesn't,
But I thought all the while 'twas a hornet."

W. S. Gilbert

There was a young man of Devizes,
Whose ears were of two different sizes;
   The one that was small
   Was of no use at all
But the other won several prizes!

An epicure dining at Crewe
Found quite a large mouse in the stew;
   Said the waiter, "Don't shout
   And wave it about
Or the rest will be wanting one too!"

🌿

There was a young fellow named Fisher,
Who was fishing for fish in a fissure,
   When a cod with a grin
   Pulled the fisherman in . . .
Now they're fishing the fissure for Fisher.

The sermon our Pastor Rt. Rev.
Began, may have had a rt. clev.,
   But his talk, though consistent,
   Kept the end so far distant
That we left since we felt he mt. nev.

※

Evangeline Alice Du Bois
Committed a dreadful *faux pas.*
   She loosened a stay
   In her decollete,
Exposing her *je ne sais quoi.*

A girl who weighed many an oz.
Used language I dare not pronoz.
   For a fellow unkind
   Pulled her chair out behind
Just to see (so he said) if she'd boz.

A tutor who tooted the flute
Tried to tutor two tooters to toot.
  Said the two to the tutor,
  "Is it harder to toot, or
To tutor two tooters to toot?"

※

In Paris some visitors go
To see what no person should know.
  And then there are tourists,
  The purest of purists,
Who say it is quite *comme il faut.*

※

She frowned and called him Mr.
Because in sport he kr.
  And so in spite
  That very nite
This Mr. kr. sr.

※

A maiden at college, Miss Breeze,
Weighed down by B.A.'s and Lit. D's,
  Collapsed from the strain.
  Said her doctor, "It's plain
You are killing yourself by degrees."

To appreciate the following gems, the American should know a few peculiarities of British pronunciation. In England, Beauchamp is pronounced "Beecham," Sydenham rhymes with "hidden 'em," Magdalen (when it's Magdalen College) is "Maudlin," Wemyss is "Weems," Cholmondeley is "Chumly," Hampshire is familiarly called "Hants," and Salisbury was formerly known as "Sarum."

⁑

Said a bad little youngster named Beauchamp:
"Those jelly tarts, how shall I reauchamp?
　　To my parents I'd go
　　But they always say 'No,'
No matter how much I beseauchamp."

⁑

Said a man to his wife down in Sydenham,
"My trousers—where have you hydenham?
　　It's perfectly true
　　They aren't brand new,
But I foolishly left half-a-quidenham."

⁑

A beauty, a perfect divinity,
Till twenty retained her virginity.
　　The boys up at Magdalen
　　Must have been dawdlin';
It couldn't have happened at Trinity.

There was once a maiden named Cholmondeley,
Who every one said was quite colmondeley,
    Yet the maid was so shy,
    That when strangers were ny,
She always would stand around dolmondeley.

There was a young curate of Salisbury
Whose manners were quite halisbury-scalisbury.
    He would wander round Hampshire
    Without any pampshire,
Till the Vicar compelled him to walisbury.

⚜

There was a young lady named Wemyss
Who, it semyss, was afflicted with dremyss.
    She would wake in the night
    And, in terrible fright,
Shake the bemyss of the house with her scremyss.

Malapropisms

When what someone says is pertinent and to the point it may be said to be apropos. When it is the opposite of these things, it is malapropos.

In 1775, the year Richard Sheridan's comedy *The Rivals* was first presented, the world was given its model of linguistic maladroitness forevermore — the tongue-tied and muddle-headed Mrs. Malaprop. Her chronic misuse and abuse of the English language gave birth to the term *malapropism,* some choice examples of which are offered below.

Strategy is when you are out of ammunition but keep right on firing so that the enemy won't know.

※

If your father was alive, he'd be turning over in his grave.

※

Your whole fallacy is wrong!

※

Gender in English tells us if a man is male, female, or neuter.

Malapropisms

Don't pay any attention to him—don't even ignore him!

※

The driver swerved to avoid missing the jaywalker.
Leo Rosten

※

He gets up at six o'clock in the morning no matter what
time it is. *Leo Rosten*

※

An oral contract isn't worth the paper it's written on.
Samuel Goldwyn

※

Don't blame God; He's only human. *Leo Rosten*

※

Every man loves his native land whether he was born
there or not. *Thomas Fitch*

※

Let us be happy and live within our means, even if we
have to borrow money to do it with.
Artemus Ward

※

You can observe a lot by watching. *Yogi Berra*

Rome is full of fallen arches.

※

You've no idea what a poor opinion I have of myself,
and how little I deserve it.　　　　*W. S. Gilbert*

※

God bless the Holy Trinity.
　　*A placard which actually led a parade of devout
　　Catholics some years ago in Dublin.*

The climate of the Sahara is such that its inhabitants
　have to live elsewhere.

※

I don't want any yesmen around me. I want everyone
　to tell me the truth—even though it costs him his
　job.　　　　*Samuel Goldwyn*

Malapropisms

No one goes to that restaurant anymore; it's too crowded.
                                                Yogi Berra

※

We're overpaying him, but he's worth it.
                                        Samuel Goldwyn

※

A lot of people my age are dead at the present time.
                                            Casey Stengel

※

Washington's farewell address was Mount Vernon.
                                            Leo Rosten

※

There's a dirge of good music on the radio.

※

Let's not downgrade this up.

※

Get on your bicycle and run like crazy.

※

Gentlemen, you may include me out.
                                        Samuel Goldwyn

Newspaper Boners

From a Gettysburg paper:

Blend sugar, flour and salt. Add egg and milk, cook until creamy in double boiler. Stir frequently. Add rest of ingredients. Mix well, serve chilled.

Funeral services will be held Thursday afternoon at 2 o'clock.

From the Boston Globe:

The House of Representatives complied by voting enough funds to hide 15 additional state troopers.

Newspaper Boners

From the Philadelphia Inquirer:
    After viewing the headless, armless and legless torso, the Coroner voiced the opinion that the real-estate agent had been slain.

※

From Tire Topics:
    To acquaint employees with Mansfield Tire's group of general foremen, we will try to report the personal histories of these important clogs in our plant machinery.

※

From the Hollywood, Cal. Citizen-News:
    One can peek in most any evening on this home-loving young actress and find her cuddled up in an easy chair with a good boob before a crackling log fire.

※

From the Harrisburg, Pa. News:
    Television Station WHP was off a matter of minutes, but the relief was short-lived.

※

From the Coos Bay-North Bend, Ore. World:
    Mrs. MacIvor has urged that all parents attend this meeting and bring the youngsters and other problems.

From the Grand Rapids, Mich. Press:
Mr. M--- visited the school yesterday and lectured on "Destructive Pests!" A large number were present.

From the Waco News-Tribune:
The district game warden filed four complaints, charging illegal fishing in Judge J. J. Padgett's court.

※

From the Idaho Statesman:
After Governor Baldridge watched the lion perform, he was taken to Main Street and fed twenty-five pounds of raw meat in front of the Fox Theater.

※

From a Louisiana newspaper:
The ladies of the Cherry Street Church have dis-

carded clothing of all kinds. Call at 44 North Cherry Street for inspection.

⁂

From a book review in the Fairmont West Virginian:
The book is nicely printed and contains few typographical errors; however, it is strange that the proo readers should rave permitted "Lay on Mac-Duff" to come out "Law on Macduff."

⁂

From the Tulsa, Okla. Daily World:
The author of *Forever Amber*, Kathleen Winsor, has written another book *Star Money*, that is called a "20th-century Amber," and is supposed to out-smell the two million copies of the first book.

⁂

From the Malone, N.Y. Telegram:
William Andrews returned home yesterday from the hospital, where his left leg was placed in a cast following a fracture of the right ankle.

⁂

From a Rifle, Colo. paper:
Mr. and Mrs. M--- R--- of Denver announce the birth of a small 7-year-old child, who didn't give his name.

From the Warsaw, Va. Northern Neck News:
Mrs. Belfield is so sappy and jolly that it is really refreshing to be with her.

※

From the Johnson City, Tenn. Press-Chronicle:
Fred V. Vance, deputy grand exhausted ruler of the Elks, will visit Johnson City on Thursday.

※

From the Grand Rapids Herald:
Miss C--- H--- reported to police the loss of $20 today. She said the money was concealed in her stocking, and the loss was discovered soon after the departure of a vacuum-cleaner salesman who had been demonstrating his line.

※

From a Nebraska weekly:
The spacious home of Judge and Mrs. Woodbury was the scene of a beautiful wedding last evening when their youngest daughter, Dorothy, was joined in holy deadlock to Mr. Wilkie.

※

From the Rochester Times Union, an advertisement for a radio program:
Hear Mr. Blank. The complete dope on the weather.

From a Jefferson City, Mo. paper:

Columbia, Tenn., which calls itself the largest outdoor mule market in the world, held a mule parade yesterday headed by the Governor.

※

From the Norwood, Ohio Enterprise:

Marjorie Evans was slightly bruised Monday afternoon when a car struck her in front of the bank. George Baker, the driver, picked her up, and feeling her all over to make sure no bones were broken, insisted on taking her home where he could make a closer examination.

※

From a Watertown, Mass. church bulletin:

Irving Jones and Jessie Brown were married on Oct. 24. So ends a friendship that began in school days.

From House & Garden:

Nothing gives a greater variety to the appearance of a house then a few undraped widows.

From the Halstead, Kans. Independent:

Mrs. E. Peterson was hostess to the Book-review Group Monday evening. Mrs. V. Chesky reviewed the book, *Three Little Pigs Stayed Home*. There were 19 present.

From the Lincoln, Neb. State Journal:

Several deer hunters in the northwoods area in the past week have been shot at by mistake for wild animals lighting cigars.

From the Omaha Sunday World-Herald:

Gene Autry is better after being kicked by a horse.

Newspaper Boners

From the Ootlewah, Tenn. Times:
Our paper carried the notice last week that Mr. Herman Ogle is a defective in the police force. This was a typographical error. Mr. Jones is, of course, a detective in the police farce.

❊

From a New York paper:
The bride was gowned in white lace. The bridesmaids' gowns were punk.

❊

From a McConnelsville, Ohio paper:
He told police that one of the men menaced him with a wench while the other covered him with a revolver.

❊

From a Wilmington, N.C. paper:
Bathing in the Easter dew, these people believe, will make them beautiful and guard them against all ham for the rest of the year.

❊

From the Columbus Dispatch:
Recovering from a head injury and shock caused by coming in contact with a live wife, Arthur E--- left Mercy Hospital Wednesday.

From a Kalamazoo paper:

Nudism would be bared in Michigan under a bill introduced in the house Wednesday.

From the Bonner Springs, Kans. Chieftain:

The song fest was hell at the Methodist church Wednesday.

※

From an El Paso paper:

W. M. McG--- lost a finger when a poisoned dog to which he was administering an anecdote bit him.

※

From the Worcester, Mass. Sunday Telegram:

State Senator Ernest A. Johnson, seeking re-election said, "I have made no wild promises, except one—honest government."

From the Boston News Bureau:
No other trains run so far for so long a distance as the "Florida Special."

※

From a Kansas City paper:
The bride is approximately eighteen feet wide from buttress to buttress.

※

From the Martinsburg, W.Va. Journal:
With 23½ pints, the two ladies were high players in four tables of duplicate bridge.

From the Greensboro, N.C. Record:
The slightly built general, with four rows of robbins on his chest, took the witness chair.

From the Los Angeles, Calif. News:

Fog and smog rolled over Los Angeles today, closing two airports and slowing snails to a traffic pace.

※

From the Kingsport, Tenn. Times:

The All-Girl Orchestra was rather weak in the bras section.

From the Honolulu Star-Bulletin:

A well-known beauty expert says that beauty is not a question of age. It is making the best of one's good paints.

※

From the Washington Post:

Adjacent to the library is another completely equipped lovatory.

Parodies

"Imitation is the sincerest form of flattery," wrote Charles Caleb Colton in the early 19th century. The parodies which follow are among the cleverest ever penned in the English language. Utterly delightful, all of them were written over half a century ago; and all of them have withstood the onslaught of time. The charm of these pieces has never withered.

THE POETS AT TEA

After Macaulay, who made it—

Pour, varlet, pour the water,
   The water steaming hot!
A spoonful for each man of us,
   Another for the pot!
We shall not drink from amber,
   Nor Capuan slave shall mix
For us the snows of Athos
   With port at thirty-six;
Whiter than snow the crystals,
   Grown sweet 'neath tropic fires,
More rich the herbs of China's field,
The pasture-lands more fragrance yield;
For ever let Britannia wield
   The tea-pot of her sires!

After Tennyson, who took it hot—

I think that I am drawing to an end:
For on a sudden came a gasp for breath,
And stretching of the hands, and blinded eyes,
And a great darkness falling on my soul.
O Hallelujah! . . . Kindly pass the milk.

After Swinburne, who let it get cold—

As the sin that was sweet in the sinning
    Is foul in the ending thereof,
As the heat of the summer's beginning
    Is past in the winter of love:
O purity, painful and pleading!
    O coldness, ineffably gray!
Oh, hear us, our handmaid unheeding,
    And take it away!

After Cowper, who thoroughly enjoyed it—

The cosy fire is bright and gay,
The merry kettle boils away
        And hums a cheerful sing.
I sing the saucer and the cup;
Pray, Mary, fill the tea-pot up,
        And do not make it strong.

Parodies

After Browning, who treated it allegorically—

Tut! Bah! We take as another case—
   Pass the bills on the pills on the window-sill; notice
     the capsule
(A sick man's fancy, no doubt, but I place
   Reliance on trade-marks, Sir)—so perhaps you'll
Excuse the digression—this cup which I hold
   Light-poised—Bah, it's spilt in the bed!—well, let's
     on go—
Hold Bohea and sugar, Sir; if you were told
   The sugar was salt, would the Bohea be Congo?

After Wordsworth, who gave it away—

"Come, little cottage girl, you seem
   To want my cup of tea;
And will you take a little cream?
   Now tell the truth to me."

She had a rustic, woodland grin,
   Her cheek was soft as silk,
And she replied, "Sir, please put in
   A little drop of milk."

"Why, what put milk into your head?
   'Tis cream my cows supply";
And five times to the child I said,
   "Why, pig-head, tell me, why?"

"You call me pig-head," she replied;
  "My proper name is Ruth.
I called that milk"—she blushed with pride—
  "You bade me speak the truth."

After Poe, who got excited over it—

Here's a mellow cup of tea, golden tea!
What a world of rapturous thought its fragrance brings
    to me!
  Oh, from out the silver cells
  How it wells!
  How it smells!
Keeping tune, tune, tune
To the tintinnabulation of the spoon.
And the kettle on the fire
Boils its spout off with desire,

With a desperate desire
And a crystalline endeavour
Now, now to sit, or never,
On the top of the pale-faced moon,
But he always came home to tea, tea, tea, tea, tea,
    Tea to the n—th.

After Rossetti, who took six cups of it—

The lilies lie in my lady's bower
  (O weary mother, drive the cows to roost),
They faintly droop for a little hour;
My lady's head droops like a flower.

She took the porcelain in her hand
  (O weary mother, drive the cows to roost),
She poured; I drank at her command;
Drank deep, and now—you understand!
  (O weary mother, drive the cows to roost),

After Burns, who liked it adulterated—

  Weel, gin ye speir, I'm no inclined,
  Whusky or tay—to state my mind,
    Fore ane or ither;
  For, gin I tak the first, I'm fou,
  And gin the next, I'm dull as you,
    Mix a' thegither.

After Walt Whitman, who didn't stay
more than a minute—

One cup for my self-hood,
Many for you. Allons, camerados, we will drink to-
    gether,
O hand-in-hand! That tea-spoon, please, when you've
    done with it.
What butter-colour'd hair you've got. I dont' want to
    be personal.
All right, then, you needn't. You're a stale-cadaver.
Eighteen-pence if the bottles are returned.
Allons, from all bat-eyed formula.

Barry Pain

☀

IF I SHOULD DIE TO-NIGHT

If I should die to-night
And you should come to my cold corpse and say,
Weeping and heartsick o'er my lifeless clay—
    If I should die to-night
And you should come in deepest grief and woe—
And say: "Here's that ten dollars that I owe,"
        I might arise in my large white cravat
        And say, "What's that?"
        If I should die to-night
And you should come to my cold corpse and kneel,
Clasping my bier to show the grief you feel,

164

I say, if I should die to-night
And you should come to me, and there and then
Just even hint 'bout paying me that ten,
        I might arise the while,
        But I'd drop dead again.

Ben King

☙

THE HIGHER PANTHEISM IN A NUTSHELL

One who is not, we see; but one, whom we see not, is;
Surely, this is not that; but that is assuredly this.

What, and wherefore, and whence: for under is over
    and under;
If thunder could be without lightning, lightning could
    be without thunder.

Doubt is faith in the main; but faith, on the whole, is
    doubt;
We cannot believe by proof; but could we believe with-
    out?

Why, and whither, and how? for barley and rye are not
    clover;
Neither are straight lines curves; yet over is under and
    over.

One and two are not one; but one and nothing is two;
Truth can hardly be false, if falsehood cannot be true.

Parallels all things are; yet many of these are askew;
You are certainly I; but certainly I am not you.

One, whom we see not, is; and one, who is not, we see;
Fiddle, we know is diddle; and diddle, we take it, is
    dee.   *Algernon Swinburne*

※

AFTER LONGFELLOW

He killed the noble Mudjokivis.
Of the skin he made him mittens,
Made them with the fur side inside,
Made them with the skin side outside.
He, to get the warm side inside,
Put the inside skin side outside;
He, to get the cold side outside,
Put the warm side fur side inside.
That's why he put the fur side inside,
Why he put the skin side outside,
Why he turned them inside outside.

※

FLU-ZEE

A bunch of germs were hitting it up
In a bronchial saloon.
Two bugs on the edge of the larynx
Were jazzing a hay-feverish tune.
While back of the teeth in a solo game
Sat dangerous Dan Kerchoo.
And watching his pulse was his queen of the wultz,
The Lady that's known as Flu.

PARODY ON POPE

Why has not man a collar and a log?
For this plain reason—man is not a dog.
Why is not man served up with sauce in dish?
For this plain reason—man is not a fish.

Sydney Smith

MARY HAD A LITTLE LAMB

Oh, Mary had a little lamb regarding whose cuticular
The fluff exterior was white and kinked in each
    particular.
On each occasion when the lass was seen
    perambulating,
The little quadruped likewise was there a gallivanting.

One day it did accompany her to the knowledge
    dispensary,
Which to every rule and precedent was recklessly
    contrary.

Immediately whereupon the pedagogue superior
Exasperated, did eject the lamb from the interior.

Then Mary, on beholding such performance arbitrary,
Suffused her eyes with saline drops from glands called
    lachrymary,
And all the pupils grew thereat tumultuously hilarious,
And speculated on the case with wild conjectures
    various.

"What makes the lamb love Mary so?" the scholars
    asked the teacher.
He paused a moment, then he tried to diagnose the
    creature.
"Oh pecus amorem Mary habit omnia temporum."
"Thanks, teacher dear," the scholars cried, and awe
    crept darkly o'er 'em.

Anonymous

THE PURPLE COW

At the end of the nineteenth century, there appeared
in a San Francisco periodical called the *Lark* a poem
entitled "The Purple Cow." Written by one of the
Lark's editors, Gelett Burgess, the whimsical verse
caught on immediately, and proved to be Burgess'
best-known work, though he continued to write for
nearly fifty years more. "The Purple Cow" was so popular a piece of nonsense that it inspired a gaggle of imi-
tations and parodies, the best of these by Carolyn Wells.

Below, we offer Burgess' original, followed by Miss

Wells' conceptions of how several well-known poets would have treated the subject of "The Purple Cow."

Mr. Burgess:

> I never saw a Purple Cow,
> I never hope to see one;
> But I can tell you, anyhow,
> I'd rather see than be one.

Carolyn Wells' Parodies:

JOHN KEATS:

A cow of purple is a joy forever.
Its loveliness increases. I have never
Seen this phenomenon. Yet ever keep
A brave lookout; lest I should be asleep
When she comes by. For, though I would not be one,
I've oft imagined 'twould be joy to see one.

WILLIAM WORDSWORTH:

> She dwelt among the untrodden ways
>   Beside the springs of Dee;
> A Cow whom there were few to praise
>   And very few to see.
>
> A violet by a mossy stone
>   Greeting the smiling East
> Is not so purple, I must own,
>   As that erratic beast.

She lived unknown, that Cow, and so
   I never chanced to see;
But if I had to be one, oh,
   The difference to me!

HENRY WADSWORTH LONGFELLOW:

The day is done, and the darkness
   Falls from the wing of night
As ballast is wafted downward
   From an air-ship in its flight.

I dream of a purple creature
   Which is not as kine are now;
And resembles cattle only
   As Cowper resembles a cow.

Such cows have power to quiet
   Our restless thoughts and rude;
They come like the Benedictine
   That follows after food.

LORD TENNYSON:

Ask me no more. A cow I fain would see
   Of purple tint, like to a sun-soaked grape—
   Of purple tint, like royal velvet cape—
But such a creature I would never be—
   Ask me no more.

JOHN MILTON:

Hence, vain, deluding cows.
  The herd of folly, without colour bright,
  How little you delight,
  Or fill the Poet's mind, or songs arouse!
  But, hail! thou goddess gay of feature!
  Hail, divinest purple creature!
  Oh, Cow, thy visage is too bright,
  To hit the sense of human sight.
  And though I'd like, just once, to see thee,
  I never, never, never'd be thee!

ROBERT BROWNING:

  All that I know
    Of a certain Cow
  Is it can throw,
    Somewhere, somehow,
  Now a dart of red,
    Now a dart of blue
  (That makes purple, 'tis said).
    I would fain see, too.
This Cow that darkles the red and the blue!

PERCY BYSSHE SHELLEY:

  Hail to thee, blithe spirit!
  Cow thou never wert;
  But in life to cheer it
  Playest thy full part
In purple lines of unpremeditated art.

171

The pale purple colour
　　Melts around thy sight
　　Like a star, but duller,
　　　In the broad daylight.
I'd see thee, but I would not be thee if I might.

　　We look before and after
　　　At cattle as they browse;
　　Our most hearty laughter
　　　Something sad must rouse.
Our sweetest songs are those that tell of Purple Cows.

DANTE GABRIEL ROSSETTI:

The Purple Cow strayed in the glade;
　(Oh, my soul! but'the milk is blue!)
She strayed and strayed and strayed and strayed
　(And I wail and I cry Wa-hoo!)

I've never seen her—nay, not I;
　(Oh, my soul! but the milk is blue!)
Yet were I that Cow I should want to die.
　(And I wail and I cry Wa-hoo!)
But in vain my tears I strew.

THOMAS GRAY:

The curfew tolls the knell of parting day,
　The lowing herd winds slowly o'er the lea;
I watched them slowly wend their weary way,

172

But, ah, a Purple Cow I did not see.
Full many a cow of purplest ray serene
Is haply grazing where I may not see;
Full many a donkey writes of her, I ween,
But neither of these creatures would I be.

EDGAR ALLAN POE:

Open then I flung a shutter,
And, with many a flirt and flutter,
In there stepped a Purple Cow which gayly tripped
around my floor.
Not the least obeisance made she,
Not a moment stopped or stayed she,
But with a mien of chorus lady perched herself above
my door.
On a dusty bust of Dante perched and sat above my
door.
And that Purple Cow unflitting
Still is sitting—still is sitting
On that dusty bust of Dante just above my chamber
door,
And her horns have all the seeming
Of a demon's that is screaming,
And the arc-light o'er her streaming
Casts her shadow on the floor.
And my soul from out that pool of Purple shadow on
the floor,
Shall be lifted Nevermore!

ALGERNON SWINBURNE:

Oh, Cow. of rare rapturous vision,
  Oh, purple, impalpable Cow,
Do you browse in a Dream Field Elysian
  Are you purpling pleasantly now?
By the side of wan waves do you languish?
  Or in the lithe lush of the grove?
While vainly I search in my anguish,
  O Bovine of mauve!

Despair in my bosom is sighing,
  Hope's star has sunk sadly to rest;
Though cows of rare sorts I am buying,
  Not one breathes a balm to my breast.
Oh, rapturous rose-crowned occasion,
  When I such a glory might see!
But a cow of a purple persuasion
  I never would be.

RUDYARD KIPLING:

In the old ten-acre pasture,
  Lookin' eastward toward a tree,
There's a Purple Cow a-settin'
  And I know she thinks of me.
For the wind is in the gum-tree,
  And the hay is in the mow,
And the cow-bells are a-calling
  "Come and see a Purple Cow!"

But I am not going now,
Not at present, anyhow,

For I am not fond of purple, and
   I can't abide a cow;
   No, I shall not go to-day,
   Where the Purple Cattle play.
   But I think I'd rather see one
   Than to be one, anyhow.

JAMES WHITCOMB RILEY:

There, little Cow, don't cry!
   You are brindle and brown, I know.
     And with wild, glad hues
     Of reds and blues,
   You never will gleam and glow.
But though not pleasing to the eye
There, little Cow, don't cry, don't cry.

Riposte

Ah, yes, I wrote the "Purple Cow"—
   I'm sorry, now, I wrote it!
But I can tell you, anyhow,
   I'll kill you if you quote it.

Gelett Burgess

Prize Insults

You have a bad habit . . . *you breathe!*

※

Don't go away mad . . . *just go away!*

※

THINK! *It may be a new experience!*

※

You can't be two-faced . . . *or you wouldn't be wearing the one you've got!*

※

Don't think it hasn't been pleasant to meet you . . . *because it hasn't!*

※

Why be difficult, when with just a little more effort you can be impossible!

※

What's on your mind? *If you will forgive the overstatement!*

※

You're certainly trying . . . *very* trying!

The sooner I never see your face again, the better it will be for both of us when we meet.

※

You should go a long way . . . *and the sooner the better.*

※

I could grow to dislike you intensely . . . *but I'm not even going to bother.*

※

If you have a minute to spare, tell me all you know.

※

When I think of you I know it's not the heat—*it's the stupidity!*

Go jump into the ocean and pull a wave over your head.

If a horse had your brains, he'd still be a horse.

※

Your visit has climaxed an already dull day.

※

Why don't you come over and have dinner . . . *If you don't mind imposing!*

※

You've got a brain . . . *but it hasn't reached your head.*

※

I'm not in the habit of forgetting faces, but in your case I will make an exception.

You're a swell guy—*and you have a head to match!*

I'd like to help you out . . . *Which way did you come in?*

※

A day away from you is like a month in the country.

※

There is something about you that I like . . . *but you spent it.*

※

I couldn't warm up to you even if we were cremated together.

※

I can't think what I'll do without you, but it's worth a try.

※

Next time you pass my house, I'll appreciate it.

※

I wouldn't engage in a battle of wits with you. I never attack anyone who is unarmed.

※

I'm really pleased to see you're back, particularly after seeing your face.

※

You should have lived in the Dark Ages . . . *you look so horrible in the light!*

You've missed so many opportunities . . . TO BE QUIET!

※

If you ever need a friend . . . buy a dog.

※

There's only one thing that you get easily—*confused!*

※

If you're so smart, why ain't you rich?

※

"I've had a wonderful evening, but this wasn't it."

※

Brains aren't everything. In fact, in your case they're *nothing.*

※

I see you've got a new position . . . *now you're standing up!*

※

I wish you were somebody, so you could make a comeback.

※

You have all the possibilities of becoming a complete stranger.

Puns

Puns have been decried by some purer-than-thous as the lowest form of humor, but we agree with Edgar Allan Poe who wrote: "Of puns it has been said that those who most dislike them are those who are least able to utter them."

In any case, puns have been the darling of the literati for as far back as goeth the memory of man. Even Queen Elizabeth allegedly succumbed to the temptation when she told Lord of Burleigh:

"Ye be burly, my Lord of Burleigh, but ye shall make less stir in our realm than my Lord of Leicester."

Other well-known personalities who have contributed to the lore of pundom, are:

GROUCHO MARX: When shooting elephants in Africa, I found the tusks very difficult to remove; but in Alabama, the Tusca-loosa.

F. P. ADAMS: Take care of your peonies and the dahlias will take care of themselves.

S. J. PERELMAN: Doctor, I've got Bright's disease and he's got mine.

SYDNEY SMITH: (upon observing two housewives yelling at each other across a courtyard) These women will never agree, for they are arguing from different premises.

PETER DE VRIES: The things my wife buys at auction are keeping me baroque.

F. P. ADAMS: Those Spanish senoritas are a snare Andalusian.

F. P. ADAMS: A group of Basques, fleeing before the enemy, were penned into a narrow mountain pass and wiped out. Which is what comes of putting all your Basques into one exit.

JIMMY DURANTE: (after blundering into the dressing room of the operatic contralto Helen Traubel) Nobody knows the Traubel I've seen.

BENNETT CERF: A relative and namesake of Syngman Rhee, former president of South Korea, was visiting our country to learn the magazine business, and got a job on what was at that time America's most popular picture periodical. On his first assignment, however, he lost himself in the mazes of New York City, until at last a Missing Persons Bureau investigator found him in a bar and cried: "Ah, sweet Mr. Rhee of *Life*, at last I've found you!"

MAX BEERBOHM: (declining a hike to the summit of a Swiss Alp) Put me down as an anti-climb Max.

WALTER WINCHELL: (explaining why he always praised the first show of a new theatrical season) Who am I to stone the first cast?

GEORGE KAUFMAN: (concerning a young Vassar coed who had eloped) She put the heart before the course!

And here are some delights from lesser-known punsters:

JIM HAWKINS: There's a vas deferens between children and no children.

JACK THOMAS: (Title for guidebook) Paris by Night and Bidet.

PHILIP GUEDALLA: (Replying to a slanderous attack on the Church) Any stigma will do to beat a dogma.

SAM HOFFENSTEIN: A teen-age girl attributed the loss of a current boyfriend to "only a passing fanny."

Four dons were strolling along an Oxford street one evening, discussing collective nouns: a covey of quail, an exaltation of larks, etc. As they conversed, they passed four ladies of the evening. One of the dons asked, "How would you describe a group like that?"

One suggested: "A jam of tarts?"

A second offered: "A flourish of strumpets?"

A third chimed in with: "An essay of Trollope's?"

The first then countered with: "A frost of hoars?"

Then the dean, the eldest and most scholarly of the four, apparently closed the discussion with: "I wish that you gentlemen would consider 'An anthology of pros.' "

Whereupon a voice behind them broke in with: "Surely you have overlooked the obvious: 'A pride of loins.' "

At a dinner party, the hostess-mother was listening with clearly evident delight to the compliments of a Mr. Campbell, which, by the way, the English pronounce by suppressing the "p" and the "b." Her daughter on the other hand was enthusiastically flirting with a gentleman named Nathaniel. Disturbed by her daughter's marked sprightliness, the mother frowned in severe reproach. Whereupon the daughter scribbled a note on a piece of paper and handed it to her mother:

Dear Ma, don't attempt my young feelings to trammel, Nor strain at a Nat while you swallow a Campbell.

Three brothers went to Texas to begin raising cattle, but they couldn't think of an appropriate name for their ranch. They wrote to their father back in Boston, and he wrote back: "I'd call it Focus, for that's where the sun's rays meet."

At a sidewalk cafe in Paris, a man ordered a cocktail for his female companion and a glass of water for himself. Ordering a second round, he told the waiter: "The lady will have another cocktail, and I'll have more of the Seine."

"One man's Mede is another man's Persian."
"Are you Shah?"
"Sultanly."

The owner of an Indianapolis antique shop dubbed his store: "Den of Antiquity." And the inmates of the Iowa State Penitentiary refer to their domicile as "The Walled-Off Astoria."

Well, as Clifton Fadiman states, of such puns we may say that their special virtue is to be tried and found wanton. Mr. Fadiman, however, has been guilty of penning the following:

In a Skid Row saloon, the patrons often enter optimistically and leave mistyoptically.

A combined charity drive represents an effort where everyone puts all their begs into one ask-it.

A gentleman crossing the English River Mersey and noting its muddy condition remarked, "Evidently the quality of Mersey is not strained."

Bennett Cerf tells of the man who poured pickle juice down a hill just to see if dill waters run steep.

And there was the wit who complained that he was always hearing his own stories told back to him: "A plain case of the tale dogging the wag."

Speaking of dogs, there was the gentleman who came into his house dripping wet and disheveled. His sympathetic wife exclaimed, "Oh dear, it's raining cats and dogs outside!"
"You're telling me," the man replied, "I just stepped in a poodle."

The tale of the king and his fool illustrates some of the dangers of pundom. The monarch, tired of his clown, told the inveterate punster: "Unless you make a pun at once—and a good one—you shall be .hanged."

"Very well," said the fool. "Name a subject."

"Myself," said the monarch. "The king."

"The king," punned the clown, "is not a subject."

"Well then," said the king, struggling to conceal his irritation, "why do you make fun of my figure?"

"Sire," said the punster, "everyone likes to make fun at someone else's expanse."

"As to royalty," pursued the king, "why do you say that Queen Elizabeth was greater than Joan of Arc?"

"Joan of Arc was a wonder," replied the clown. "But Queen Elizabeth was a Tudor."

"Enough!" cried the king. "Hang him!"

But as the noose was drawn around the punster's neck, the king said, "I'll grant you your life on one condition: that you'll promise never to make another pun."

"I promise, your Majesty," said the jester. "No noose is good news."

So they hanged him.

And they should have hanged the perpetrators of this pun-laden conversation:

Waitress: Hawaii, sir? You must be Hungary.

Gent: Yes, Siam. I can't Rumania long, Venice lunch ready?

Waitress: I'll Russia table. What'll you Havre? Aix?

Gent: Whatever's ready, But can't Jamaica cook hurry?

Waitress: Odessa laugh! But Alaska.

Gent: And put a Cuba sugar in my Java.

Waitress: Don't you be Sicily. Sweden it yourself. I'm only here to Serbia.

Gent: Denmark my check and call the Bosphorus. I'll hope he'll Kenya. I don't Bolivia know who I am!

Waitress: Canada noise! I don't Caribbean. You sure Ararat!

Gent: Samoa your wisecracks? What's got India? D'you think this arguing Alps business? Be Nice!

Waitress: Don't Kiev me that Boulogne! Alamein do! S'pain in the neck. Pay your check and beat it. Abyssinia!

These, then, are the rhymes that try men's souls. Before we submit our own dictionary of puns, we call Mr. James Boswell for the Defense:

A good pun may be admitted among the small ex-cellencies of lively conversation.

And finally, we present this anonymous lyric dedicated to the *double-entendre*:

> A pun is the lowest form of wit,
> It does not tax the brain a bit;
> One merely takes a word that's plain
> And picks one out that sounds the same.
> Perhaps some letter may be changed
> Or others slightly disarranged,
> This to the meaning gives a twist,

Puns

Which much delights the humorist.
A sample now may help to show
The way a good pun ought to go:
"It isn't the cough that carries you off,
It's the coffin they carry you off in."

You may find the puns which follow perhaps less sophisticated, but nevertheless more uproarious.

AMAZON You can pay for the eggs, but the amazon me.

ANTIDOTES My uncle likes me very much and my antidotes on me.

ARREARS Brother and I both hate to wash in back of arrears.

AVENUE I avenue baby sitter.

AVOID Stop me if you avoid this one before.

BULLETIN My brother fought in the war and he has a bulletin his leg.

CANADA You bring the corn and I'll bring a canada best peas.

CIGARETTE Cigarette life, if you don't weaken.

CUCKOO We have a new cuckoo makes nice cake.

DAISIES Ma's always glad when school starts because Johnnie's such a nuisance the daisies at home.

DECEIT   Ma makes me wear pants with patches on deceit.

DEMURE   When people start to get rich, demure they get, demure they want.

DIABETES   That baseball team has sworn they'll either diabetes.

DIALOGUE   Insult her and you will dialogue a dog.

DUBLIN   Ireland is rich because its capital is always Dublin.

EURIPEDES   Mr. Tailor, Euripedes pants and I'll make you pay.

EXPLAIN   Please don't scramble them; I like my explain.

FALSIFY   When I put a book on my head it falsify move.

FORFEIT	The horse jumped over the cop and landed with all its forfeit on the ground.
GLADIATOR	That old hen wasn't laying any eggs, so I'm gladiator.
HISTORIAN	That's historian he's stuck with it.
JUICY	When we came through the alley, juicy what I saw?
JUSTIFY	Ma promised me a quarter justify brush my teeth.
LAZINESS	It's no wonder baby doesn't get tired—he laziness crib all day.
LILAC	He's a nice kid but he can lilac anything.
LOQUACIOUS	She bumped into me and I told her to loquacious going.
MINIATURE	Take a pill and you'll be asleep the mini-ature in bed.

MUTILATE — I could get more sleep if our cat didn't mutilate every night.

NUISANCE — I haven't seen anything nuisance I came back.

REVEREND — Teacher says if I don't study I'll be in this grade for reverend ever.

SAUSAGE — The soup was excellent, but I never sausage a steak.

SELFISH — That fish market would be just grand if it didn't make their men selfish.

SOVIET — Dinner was announced, Soviet.

SPADE — The man who digs ditches these days gets spade well for his work.

SURGEON — Willie likes his gray suit but he looks nicer with his blue surgeon.

TELEPHONY — He may have fooled you, but I can telephony.

TORONTO — When you hit the ball you have toronto first base.

UNAWARE — Every night, before I go to bed, I take off my unaware.

WIGGLE — She wears her hat all day because she's afraid her wiggle come off.

Riddles

The riddle is perhaps the oldest of all puzzles, and perhaps the most famous of all riddles is the one asked by the Sphinx:

> *What goes on four legs in the morning,*
> *on two at noon, and on three at night?*

Oedipus answered the riddle correctly, and thus became Oedipus Rex.

His solution: "Man. In infancy, he crawls; in his prime, he walks; in old age, he leans on a staff."

Another famous riddle is one that is reputed to have stumped Homer. Someone propounded these two lines to the bard:

> *What we caught we threw away;*
> *What we couldn't catch, we kept.*

The answer to this one is fleas.

It was a long time until the next classic riddle came along:

> *When is a door not a door?*

When it is ajar, naturally. What this riddle loses in classical phrasing it makes up in modern lunacy. Here are some more:

What is worse than a louse, stronger than God, and if you eat it you die?

Nothing. What is stronger than God? Nothing. What is worse than a louse? Nothing. And if you eat nothing—you die.

What's the difference between a bird with one wing and a bird with two wings?

A difference of a pinion.

I am the center of gravity, hold a capital situation in Vienna, and as I am foremost in every victory, am allowed by all to be invaluable. Always out of tune, yet ever in voice; invisible, though clearly seen in the midst of a river. I have three associates in vice, and could name three who are in love with me. Still it is in vain you seek me, for I have long been in heaven, and even now lie embalmed in the grave. Who am I?

The letter V.

Four jolly men sat down to play,
And played all night till break of day;
They played for cash and not for fun,
With a separate score for every one;
Yet when they came to square accounts,
They all had made quite fair amounts!
Can you this paradox explain?
If no one lost, how could all gain?

194

They were musicians in a dance orchestra.

What is the difference among a king's son, a monkey's mother, a bald head, and an orphan?

A king's son is an heir apparent, a monkey's mother is a hairy parent, a bald head has no hair apparent, and an orphan has nary a parent.

Why are golfers not using clubs any longer?

Because they're long enough now.

What has four wheels and flies?

A garbage truck.

What did Cleopatra say when Mark Antony asked if she was true to him?

Omar Khayyam.

What is a crick?

The noise made by a Japanese camera.

Who was Alexander Graham Bell Pulaski?

The first telephone Pole.

What do they call the Englishman who builds ten boats a month?

Sir Launchalot.

What kind of a waiter never accepts a tip?

A dumb waiter.

What do ducks do when they fly upside down?

They quack up.

What's black and white and hides in a cave?

A zebra that owes money.

What does a 200-pound mouse say?

Here, kitty, kitty.

What color is a burp?
Burple.

Ruthless Rhymes

The ditties below might well have been penned by the Marquis de Sade. Whoever is responsible for these shameless sentiments should at least find coal in his stocking next Christmas.

> Little Willie, in the best of sashes,
> Fell in the fire and was burned to ashes.
> By and by the room grew chilly,
> But no one liked to poke up Willie.

> *Help! Murder! Police!*
> My wife fell down in grease;
>   I laughed so hard, I fell in the lard.
> *Help! Murder! Police!*

Making toast at the fireside,
Nurse fell in the grate and died;
And what makes it ten times worse—
All the toast was burned with Nurse.

※

Little Willie hung his sister;
She was dead before we missed her.
Willie's always up to tricks!
Ain't he cute? He's only six!

※

Pity now poor Mary Ames,
Blinded by her brother James;
Hot nails in her eyes he poked—
I ne'er saw Mary more provoked.

※

In the deep, deep drinking-well
    Which the plumber built her,
Dear Aunt Eliza fell—
    We must buy a filter.

※

Baby Bobby in the tub;
Ma forgot to place the plug;
Oh what sorrow! Oh what pain!
There goes Bobby down the drain!

Sam had spirits naught could check,
   And today, at breakfast, he
Broke his baby sister's neck,
   So he shan't have jam for tea!

※

Little Willie, mean as hell,
Pushed his sister in the well,
Mother said, while drawing water,
"My it's hard to raise a daughter!"

※

Father heard his children scream,
So he threw them in the stream;
Saying, as he drowned the third,
"Children should be seen, *not* heard!"

※

O'er the rugged mountain's brow
   Clara threw the twins she nursed,
And remarked, "I wonder now
   Which will reach the bottom first?"

※

Auntie, did you feel no pain
   Falling from that apple tree?
Would you do it, please, again?
   'Cos my friend here didn't see.

I had written to Aunt Maud,
Who was on a trip abroad,
When I heard she'd died of cramp—
Just too late to save the stamp.

※

Little Willie, on his bike,
Through the village took a hike.
Mrs. Thompson blocked the walk;
She will live, but still can't talk.

※

Little Willie, home from school,
Where he'd learned the Golden Rule,
Said, "If I eat up this cake
Sis won't have a stomach-ache."

※

Little Will, with father's gun,
Punctured grandma, just for fun.
Mother frowned at the merry lad:
It was the last shell father had.

※

INDIFFERENCE

When Grandmamma fell off the boat
And couldn't swim, and wouldn't float,
Matilda just stood by and smiled.
I very nearly slapped the child.

COMPENSATION

Weep not for little Léonie,
Abducted by a French *marquis*.
Though loss of honor was a wrench,
Just think how it improved her French.

Willie saw some dynamite,
Couldn't understand it quite;
Curiosity never pays;
It rained Willie seven days.

Willie scalped his baby brother,
  Left him lying hairless;
"Willie," said his worried mother,
  "You are getting careless."

Willie, hitting at a ball,
Lined one down the school-house hall.
Through his door came Dr. Hill.
Several teeth are missing still.

Father, I regret to state,
Cut his daughters up for bait,
We miss them when it's time to dine,
But father's fish taste simply fine.

※

Little Willie lit a rocket
Which his Pa had in his pocket.
Next day he told Uncle Dan,
"Papa is a traveling man."

※

Willie poisoned father's tea;
Father died in agony.
Mother came, and looked quite vexed:
"Really, Will," she said, "what next?"

※

Little Willie on the track
    Heard the engine squeal.
Now the engine's coming back;
    They're scraping Willie off the wheel.

※

Willie's Pa, I grieve to state,
Came home from the lodge quite late.
When he tottered Willie cried,
"Look at Papa! He's off-side!"

Willie as the fire burned low,
Gave it a terrific blow.
Grandpa's beard got in the draft;
Dear me, how the firemen laughed!

※

Willie in the cauldron fell;
  See the grief on mother's brow!
Mother loved her darling well;
  Darling's quite hard-boiled by now.

※

Willie fell down the elevator—
Wasn't found till six days later.
Then the neighbors sniffed, "Gee whizz!
What a spoiled child Willie is!"

Show Me

Show me where Stalin is buried—and I'll show you a Communist plot.

⁂

Show me the first President's dentures—and I'll show you the George Washington Bridge.

Show me a pharaoh who ate crackers in bed—and I'll show you a crummy mummy.

⁂

Show me a squirrel's nest—and I'll show you the Nutcracker Suite.

Show Me

Show me Santa's helpers—and I'll show you subordinate clauses.

※

Show me a famous surgeon—and I'll show you a big operator.

※

Show me a cat that just ate a lemon—and I'll show you a sourpuss.

※

Show me a cross between a fox and a mink—and I'll show you a fink.

※

Show me a one-word commercial—and I'll show you an adverb.

※

Show me a famous composer's liquor cabinet—and I'll show you Beethoven's Fifth.

※

Show me Eve's perfume—and I'll show you an Adam balm.

※

Show me a man convicted of two crimes—and I'll show you a compound sentence.

※

Show me a singing beetle—and I'll show you a humbug.

Show me two dozen satisfied rabbits—and I'll show you 24 carats.

※

Show me a burned-out post office—and I'll show you a case of blackmail.

※

Show me a cross between a cannon and a bell—and I'll show you a boomerang.

※

Show me a young lad's bed—and I'll show you a boy-cott.

※

Show me a wily halfback with a knack for sketching—and I'll show you an artful dodger.

※

Show me a workman who dismantles a roof—and I'll show you an eavesdropper.

※

Show me a baker who ran out of custard—and I'll show you a humble pie.

※

Show me a cross between a mule and a fox—and I'll show you a fool.

Show Me

Show me a monarch who takes tea at four—and I'll show you the King's English.

⚜

Show me a fowl with an artificial leg—and I'll show you a lame duck amendment.

⚜

Show me a stolen sausage—and I'll show you a missing link.

⚜

Show me a healed shaving scar—and I'll show you an old nick.

⚜

Show me a frog on a lily pad—and I'll show you a toad-stool.

⚜

Show me a man who's afraid of Christmas—and I'll show you a Noel Coward.

⚜

Show me a magician's notebook—and I'll show you a spellbinder.

⚜

Show me a golden wedding anniversary—and I'll show you high fidelity.

Show me a fillibustering senator—and I'll show you a figure of speech.

Show me a diminutive barber—and I'll show you a shortcut.

Show me a swine in the rain—and I'll show you hog-wash.

Show me a girl who shuns the miniskirt—and I'll show you hemlock.

Show me a toddler caught playing in the mud—and I'll show you grime and punishment.

Show me a tall beachcomber—and I'll show you a long-shoreman.

Show me a low-cut dress—and I'll show you a cold shoulder.

※

Show me a mixture of fennel and tobasco—and I'll show you a fiasco.

※

Show me a gang of beggars—and I'll show you a rag-time band.

※

Show me a flagellant witch—and I'll show you goulash.

※

Show me an arrogant insect—and I'll show you a cocky roach.

※

Show me a manhole at a street intersection—and I'll show you a connoisseur.

※

Show me Mohammed Ali's safe-deposit box—and I'll show you Cassius' Cash Can.

※

Show me a football player with keen intuition—and I'll show you a hunchback.

※

Show me a violin maker—and I'll show you a man with guts.

Spoonerisms

William Archibald Spooner was a British clergyman who lived from 1844 to 1930. He was a very nice man, but probably a little self-conscious. Very often, when he was speaking or lecturing, he would unwittingly switch his words around. His mistakes, which caused much laughter, have made him immortal.

On one occasion, Spooner, intending to announce to his congregation that they were about to sing the hymn "From Greenland's Icy Mountains," declared the title to be "From Iceland's Greasy Mountains."

This kind of mistake, switching around letters and thus changing the words, is called a spoonerism. Here are some others:

> Shores of skells were fired in a bittle batter.
>
> The picture is available in color and whack and blight.
>
> Shellout falters.
>
> He is a newted nose analyst.
>
> President Hoobert Heever.
>
> The Duck and Dooches of Windsor.
>
> The sporks and foons.

You hissed my mystery lectures.

The kankering kongs.

A blushing crow.

The tons of soil.

His sin twister.

Outside, a roaring pain is falling.

I am grattered and flatified.

A half-warmed fish.

"Kinquering Kongs Their Titles Take"

"Is it kisstomary to cuss the bride?"

It is reported that Spooner once referred to Queen Victoria as "our queer old dean."

Some vaudeville comic dreamed up this Spooneristic routine for a drunk:

"Now missen, lister, all I had was tee martoonis. Sough I theem under the affluence of inkahol, I'm not palf as hickled—half as packled—as thinkle peep—as theeple pink I am."

Perhaps the most famous spoonerism is apocryphal. The story goes that the good reverend walked over to a lady in church and said, "Mardon me, padam, but this pie is occupewed. May I sew you to another sheet?"

Triple Platform

Among the memorials of the sectional conflict of 1861-65 is an American platform which was arranged to suit all parties of that day. The first column is the *Secession* platform; the second, the *Abolition* platform; and the whole, read across in one line, presents the Democratic party platform of that particular era.

Hurrah for	The Old Union
Secession	Is a curse
We fight for	The Constitution
The Confederacy	Is a league with hell
We love	Free speech
The rebellion	Is treason
We glory in	A Free Press
Separation	Will not be tolerated
We fight not for	The Negro's freedom
Reconstruction	Must be obtained
We must succeed	At every hazard
The Union	We love
We love not	The Negro
We never said	Let the Union slide
We want	The Union as it was
Foreign intervention	Is played out
We cherish	The old flag
The stars and bars	Is a flaunting lie
We venerate	The *habeas corpus*
Southern chivalry	Is hateful
Death to	Jeff Davis
Abe Lincoln	Isn't the Government
Down with	Mob law
Law and order	Shall triumph

Typographical Poetry

A typographical poem may convey its message in both word and image, content and form—or it may communicate in a bizarre shorthand which yields surprising results. Offered here are some examples of each type of typographical verse. If you have any trouble deciphering the first ditty, here's a clue: the versifier might have taken lessons from Fanny·Brice.

FUNEX?

SVFX

FUNEM?

SVFM

OK. LFMNX

⁂

I'm sorry you've been 6 o long;
    Don't b disconsol8;
But bear your ills with 42de,
    & they won't seem to gr8.

⁂

O I C

I'm in a 10der mood to-day
    & feel poetic, 2;
4 fun I'll just—off a line
    & send it off 2 u.

214

ABCD goldfish?
LMNO goldfish
OSAR 2 goldfish!

For a lark,
For a prank,
Ezra Shank
Walked a plank.
These bubbles mark

O
O
O
O
O

Where Ezra sank.

※

YYUR
YYUB
ICUR
YY4ME

215

And what mean all these mysteries to me
　　Whose life is full of indices and surds?
$x^2 + 7x + 53$
　　$= 11/3$

Lewis Carroll

My tYpust is on hor vacution,
　　My trypist's awau fpr a week,
My typudt us in hwr vscarion
　　Wgile thse danm kews plsy hude and seej.

※

A pair in a hammock
Attempted to kiss,
And in less than a jiffy
They landed like this.

LOVE'S ACROBATICS

He went out one lovely night
   To call upon a miss,
And when he reached her residence
                    this.
              like
          stairs
        up
    ran
He
Her papa met him at the door,
   He didn't see the miss.
He'll not go there again though—for
He
    ʇuǝʍ
      down
        sɹıɐʇs
          like
            ·sıɥʇ

                 Anonymous

        ✻

O, MLE, what XTC
I always feel when UIC,
I used to rave of LN'S eyes,
4 LC I gave countless sighs,
4 KT, 2, and LNR,
I was a keen competitor.
But each now's a non-NTT,
4 U XL them all UC.

217

A gentleman by the name of Charlie Leedy penned this droll observation for the *Youngstown Telegram*:

> Now, ladies in a crowded bus
> Occasion very little fuss
> Because they always cross their knees,
> Conserving space, a bit like these:
> XXXXXX
>
> But gaze upon a row of men
> And blush for shame a little when
> You see their spreading, sprawling ways
> That make them like this row of A's:
> AAAAAA

Mr. Leedy's lines prompted a number of other rhymesters to propound on the subject. Here are two of the best quatrains inspired by his verse.

> But only yesterday I rode
> Across from one whose legs were bowed;
> The best she could achieve, poor miss,
> Was something very much like this:
> VVVVVV
>
> But I wish you would tell me, please,
> How they could have been like V's.
> Unless my eyes deceive me, miss,
> Bow legs in street cars look like this:
> ( ) ( ) ( ) ( ) ( ) ( ) ( ) ( )

Whimsical Verse.

The following stanzas, offered for your delectation, range in literary merit from slight to nil. Nevertheless, many have survived through generations which, in itself, attests to their appeal.

> The savages closed around the tent;
>   The lovers trembled in the gloom;
> They knew their life was well-nigh spent,
>   They knew they faced their doom.
> He kissed the ringlets on her head,
>   He crushed her in embrace of death;
> And as he kissed her lips he said,
>   *"There's garlic on your breath!"*

Divorced are Mr. and Mrs. Howell;
He wiped their car with her guest towel.

If all the land were apple-pie,
   And all the sea were ink;
And all the trees were bread and cheese,
   What should we do for drink?

※

I often pause and wonder at fate's peculiar ways,
For nearly all our famous men were born on holidays.

This is the story of Johnny McGuire
Who ran through the town with trousers on fire.
He went to the doctor's and fainted with fright
When the doctor told him his end was in sight.

※

Here is a riddle most abstruse:
   Canst read the answer right?
Why is it that my tongue grows loose
   Only when I grow tight?

The bee is such a busy soul
It has no time for birth control;
And that is why in times like these
There are so many sons of bees.

※

Alas! the poor Hindu; he does what he kindu;
And as for his trousers, he makes his own skindu.

※

"I love the ground you walk on!" This was the tale he
told.
For they lived up the Klondike, and the ground was full
of gold!

※

I wish I were a kangaroo,
Despite his funny stances;
I'd have a place to put the junk
My girl brings to the dances.

※

They walked in the lane together,
The sky was covered with stars;
They reached the gate in silence,
He lifted down the bars.
She neither smiled nor thanked him
Because she knew not how;
For he was just a farmer's boy,
And she—a Jersey cow.

Mary Jones took her skates
 Upon the ice to frisk;
Now wasn't she a foolish girl
 Her little *

※

Yesterday upon the stair
I saw a man who wasn't there.
He wasn't there again today;
I wish to heck he'd go away.

※

I eat my peas with honey,
 I've done it all my life;
They do taste kind of funny,
 But it keeps them on the knife.

※

All right, go lie upon the beach,
To bake beyond the water's reach;
But if you're blistered when you quit,
Remember that you basked for it.

※

There was an old woman
 Who lived in a shoe
She had so many children
 Her government relief check came to $4892.

I sneezed a sneeze into the air,
It fell to earth I know not where;
But hard and cold were the looks of those
In whose vicinity I snooze.

※

She took my hand with loving care;
She took my costly flowers so rare.
She took my candy and my books!
She took my eye with meaning looks.
She took all that I could buy,
And then she took the other guy.

※

A centipede was happy quite,
  Until a frog, in fun,
Said, "Pray, which leg comes after which?"
This raised her mind to such a pitch
She lay distracted in a ditch,
  Considering how to run.

Oh, what a blamed uncertain thing
   This pesky weather is:
It blew and snew and then it thew
   And now, by jing, it friz!

I crept upstairs, my shoes in hand,
   Just as the night took wing,
And saw my wife, four steps above,
   Doing the same darned thing.

☀

Say it with flowers,
   Say it with eats
Say it with kisses,
   Say it with sweets,
Say it with jewelry,
   Say it with drink,
But always be careful
   Not to say it with ink!

He wrecked his car, he lost his job
And yet throughout his life,
He took his troubles like a man:
He blamed them on his wife.

※

How sweet to waken in the morn
  When sunbeams first begin to creep
Across the lea—and then to lie
  Right back again and go to sleep.
                    Youngstown Telegram

※

CASTING STONES

For laundresses, the soapstone;
For architects, the cornerstone;
For cooks, the puddingstone;
For soldiers, the bloodstone;
For politicians, the blarneystone;
For borrowers, the touchstone;
For policemen, the pavingstone;
For stock brokers, the curbstone;
For shoemakers, the cobblestone;
For burglers, the keystone;
For tourists, the Yellowstone;
For beauties, the peachstone;
For editors, the grindstone;
For motorists, the milestone;
For pedestrians, the tombstone.

How sweet to waken in the morn
   Without one bit of fear or doubt,
And sudden then to realize
   The furnace fire is all but out.
                  Oakland Times

※

How sweet to waken in the morn
   Without a care the mind to cumber,
Then hurry to the phone and find
   Some jerk is calling the wrong number.

※

T'was in a restaurant they met
Brave Romeo and Juliet.
He had no cash to pay his debt
So Romeo'd what Juli'et.

※

The lightning bug is brilliant,
   But it hasn't any mind;
It blunders through existence,
   With its headlight on behind.

Wisecracks

The new army rifle weighs 8.60 pounds. After you've carried it for a few hours, the decimal point drops out.

 ☀

The food in this hotel is absolutely poison—and such small portions!

 ☀

Marriage is popular because it combines the maximum of temptation with the maximum of opportunity.

G. B. Shaw

Seven days in a jeep makes one weak.

 ☀

Many a pert girl goes out to flirt and comes back *ex*-pert.

I know the King's English, and so is the Queen.

☀

A great many prominent family trees were started by grafting.

☀

Try praising your wife, even if it does frighten her at first. *Billy Sunday*

☀

Look pleasant, please. As soon as I snap the picture, you can resume your natural expression.

Every woman likes to be taken with a grain of assault.

☀

He reminds me of the man who murdered both his parents and then when sentence was about to be pronounced, pleaded for mercy on the grounds that he was an orphan.

Lincoln

❀

The race is not always to the swift, nor the battle to the strong, but that's the way to bet.

Damon Runyon

❀

A gossip is a woman with a good sense of rumor.

❀

The average man is an irrational creature who's always looking for home atmosphere in a hotel, and hotel service at home.

❀

Economy, my son, is anything your mother wants to buy.   *Fred Neher*

The only thing worse than being talked about is not being talked about.   *Oscar Wilde*

❀

Some taverns don't serve women at the bar: you have to bring your own.

❀

Money isn't everything—that is, *Confederate* money.

If all the college boys who sleep in class were placed end to end, they would be more comfortable.

⚜

The bigger the summer vacation, the harder the fall.

The cook was a good cook, as cooks go; and as cooks go, she went.

⚜

When people go to summer hotels for a change and rest, the bellboys get the change and the hotel gets the rest.

⚜

Money isn't everything—but it's ahead of whatever is in second place.

⚜

It was just a platonic friendship—play for him, tonic for her!

230

To love oneself is the beginning of a lifelong romance.
Oscar Wilde

Half the lies they tell about me aren't true.

You should study the Peerage . . . It is the best thing in fiction the English have done. *Oscar Wilde*

After a divorce, a woman feels like a new man.

Youth is a wonderful thing. What a crime to waste it on children. *G. B. Shaw*

Most women claim to be dresstitute.

There are three kinds of lies: lies, damned lies, and statistics. *Disraeli*

My sister got herself a second lieutenant—the first one got away.

All work and no play makes jack.

In the first place God made idiots. This was for practice. Then He made School Boards. *Mark Twain*

Where there's a will, there's a relative.

What can one expect of a day that begins with getting up in the morning?

People are more fun than anybody.
Dorothy Parker

Never break your bread or roll in your soup.

I was in a phone booth talking to my girl, but someone wanted to use the phone, so we had to get out.

There are several good five-cent cigars on the market, but they are sold at higher prices.

※

Getting the baby to sleep is hardest when she's about 18 years old.

※

Don't question your wife's judgment—look whom she married!

※

Courtship is the period during which the girl makes up her mind whether or not she can do any better.

※

Marriage is a romance in which the hero dies in the first chapter.

※

Thirty is a nice age for a woman—especially if she happens to be forty.

※

Lend your neighbor a garden rake and he'll come back for mower.

※

Brother started off working for peanuts until he proved his salt. Now he gets salted peanuts.

※

Immigration is the sincerest form of flattery.

A diplomat? He's the man who can convince his wife that a woman looks stout in a fur coat.

✵

Sports cars owned by Hollywood actors are so plush and powerful that their motors don't purr, they sneer.

✵

Samson had the right idea about advertising. He took two columns and brought down the house.

✵

The well-bred man steps on his cigarette so it won't burn the rug.

✵

Every man loves his native land whether he was born there or not.   *Thomas Fitch*

✵

It is not generally considered proper for the hostess to wear a T-shirt while serving tea.

✵

My mother got up every morning at 5:00 a.m. no matter what time it was.   *Sam Levenson*

✵

The trouble with being punctual is that nobody's there to appreciate it.

"Maybe they can't make you fight," said the draft
officer, "but they can take you where the fighting
is, and you can use your own judgment."

After two days in the hospital, he took a turn for the
nurse.

After eating a meal in a first-class restaurant nowadays,
you need an after-dinner mint—such as the one in
Denver.   *Irving Lazar*

If you actually look like your passport photo, you aren't
well enough to travel.

The difference between the right word and the nearly
right word is the difference between the lightning
and the lightning bug.   *Mark Twain*

A husband who is boss in his own house is probably a liar about other things, too.   *Will Rogers*

❋

A speaker who does not strike oil in ten minutes should stop boring.

❋

He was a Boy Scout until he was 16—then he became a girl scout.

❋

I do the hardest work of my whole day before breakfast —getting up.   *Bob Crosby*

❋

Her face is her fortune—and it runs into a nice figure.

❋

He reads just enough to keep himself misinformed.

❋

All the things I really like to do are either immoral, illegal or fattening.   *Alexander Woolcott*

❋

There are three major parties in the United States—the Democratic Party, the Republican Party and the cocktail party.

❋

In politics the paths of glory lead but to the gravy.

Nobody who can read is ever successful at cleaning out an attic.

※

I often quote myself. It adds spice to my conversation.
Bernard Shaw

※

In three days guests, like fish, begin to stink.
Benjamin Franklin

※

One of the greatest laborsaving inventions of today is tomorrow.

※

The best way to make a fire with two sticks is to make sure one of them is a match.   *Will Rogers*

※

If all the automobiles in the world were placed end to end it would be Sunday afternoon.

※

Never slap a man in the face—especially when he's chewing tobacco.   *Abe Martin*

※

To make a long story short, there's nothing like having the boss walk in.   *Doris Lilly*

You Tell 'Em.

You tell 'em,   BALDHEAD   *You're smooth!*

You tell 'em.   BALLOON   *You're on the up and up.*

You tell 'em,   BANK   *You're safe!*

You tell 'em,   BIBLE   *You've got the word.*

You tell 'em,   BEAN   *He's stringing you!*

You tell 'em,   CABBAGE   *You've got the head!*

You tell 'em,   CASHIER   *I'm a poor teller!*

You tell 'em,   CEILING   *It's over my head.*

You tell 'em,   CHLOROFORM   *You put 'em to sleep!*

You Tell 'Em

You tell 'em,	CLOCK	*You've got the time!*
You tell 'em,	CLOUD	*It's up to you.*
You tell 'em,	CRYSTAL	*You're on the watch!*
You tell 'em,	DENTIST	*You've got the pull!*
You tell 'em,	DOCTOR	*You've got the patience!*
You tell 'em,	DOUGH	*You're well-bred!*

You tell 'em,	ELECTRICITY	*You can shock 'em!*
You tell 'em,	ENGLISH	*You're on the ball.*
You tell 'em,	ENVELOPE	*You're well posted!*
You tell 'em,	GOLDFISH	*You've been around the globe!*
You tell 'em,	HUNTER	*I'm game.*

You tell 'em,	JUNE	*And don't July!*
You tell 'em,	LAMP	*I'm in the dark.*
You tell 'em,	MOUNTAIN	*I'm only a bluff!*
You tell 'em,	NUMBER	*You're the one.*
You tell 'em,	OPERATOR	*You've got their number!*
You tell 'em,	PIE	*You've got the crust!*
You tell 'em,	PLANE	*You're on the level.*
You tell 'em,	PLATO	*It's Greek to me!*
You tell 'em,	PRINTER	*I'm not your type!*
You tell 'em,	RAILROAD	*It's along your line.*
You tell 'em,	SIMON	*I'll Legree!*
You tell 'em,	SLEEPWALKER	*You never lie.*
You tell 'em,	TIN PAN	*It's up your alley.*
You tell 'em,	TOOTH	*You've got the nerve.*